ONE PIECE OF THE PUZZLE

A SCHOOL READINESS MANUAL

by

Barbara Carll

and

Nancy Richard

Athena Publications - Moravia, NY

Originally published in 1972 as *School Readiness -
One Piece of the Puzzle.* The New Hampshire
School Readiness Project. Title III of ESEA
International Standard Book Number: 0-932950-00-0
Library of Congress Catalog Card Number: 77-076434
Athena Publications, Moravia, NY 13118
© 1977 by Athena Publications. All rights reserved.
Revised Edition
First Athena Publications Edition
Fifth Printing 1985
Printed in the United States of America

Peggy Gunar

TABLE OF CONTENTS

STATEMENT

This manual proposes a method of alleviating the problems surrounding school entrance policy. It is the culmination of five years' work by the New Hampshire School Readiness Project funded under Title III of the Elementary and Secondary Education Act of 1965.

It would seem advisable to apply as much expertise to the child's initial entrance to school, this embarkation on the total educational career, as is now currently applied to college entrance. It is the intent of this manual to delineate ways in which a school readiness program might be implemented in schools. This manual is possible because many of the New Hampshire schools which have already instituted readiness programs have shared their mistakes and successes with us.

For many years, the criterion for school entrance has been a chronological age set by state law. Such a practice assumes that all children develop at the same rate and are ready for the same experiences at the age of six. Children, however, do not develop at the same rate. Child development specialists have found there can be a two-year spread in maturation among normal children at the age of six.

Very briefly, what is advocated is that each child be placed in school according to developmental or functioning level rather than according to chronological age. This implies the need for a developmental assessment before the child enters school. It is advocated that those children who are found developmentally young be provided with an adjusted curriculum, one suited to their developmental needs. This is usually in the form of a pre-first-grade room called a Readiness Room, a Transition Room, Pre-Primary, or other. For the sake of consistency, it will be called a Pre-First-Grade room in this manual.

The procedures put forth here and, in fact, the whole design, are offered not as the only possible ways of dealing with the problem of school entrance, but simply as one method which has been tried and found to be worth consideration. There is much yet to be learned about school readiness; this manual is an indication of where we are right now.

Although implementation of a school readiness program such as is suggested here will have a direct beneficial effect on the number of high school dropouts, retentions, emotional and learning problems, and general tone and mood within the school, it will not solve all educational problems. It is no panacea. It is an expedient which will save many children *now*. It is a change for the better which seems to cause very little upheaval for the amount of benefit derived. It is a first step. It is one piece of the large puzzle of *when, where,* and *how* to best educate children.

GLOSSARY

DEVELOPMENTAL AGE. The age at which a child is behaving as a total organism—a functioning age. A child might very well be functioning at a six, or even a seven, year-old level intellectually or in some other aspect of development, but a composite of the *whole* development might place the child at a five-year-old functioning age. Developmental age is the age where a child sustains—where the child is "grounded."

DEVELOPMENTAL EXAMINATION. A systematic series of tasks through which the child reveals a level of behavior as a total organism—where the child is now on the growth continuum.

GROWTH. Growth is used synonomously with Development. It means progress in emotional stability, intellectual maturity, and social competence, as well as physical growth. Perhaps most importantly, it means advancement of the integration process—advancement in differentiation—an increase in complexity of function.

MATURATION. The process by which each child "unfolds" according to the individual biological timetable; the process is controlled chiefly by genetic and constitutional factors.

OVERPLACEMENT. Being in over one's head—being in a school situation which is causing strain to the organism.

PRE-FIRST-GRADE. A learning environment for children who are six years old chronologically, but younger in total development. Often a grade between kindergarten and grade one. Sometimes called Readiness Room, Transition Room, Pre-Primary, or Level I.

READINESS PROGRAM. A change in the traditional school organization whereby children are placed in first grade by their developmental ages rather than their chronological ages. Provision is usually made for those children who are young in development to have a Pre-First-Grade program.

SCHOOL READINESS. Ability to cope with school environment physically, socially, and emotionally, as well as academically, without undue stress, and to sustain in that environment.

SCHOOL SUCCESS. Achievement without undue stress. Learning with enough spirit and energy left over to develop into a well-integrated person.

SKEWED DEVELOPMENT. Lopsided, distorted development. Usually caused by pushing one aspect of development ahead of the others; for instance, pushing intellectual growth with little regard for the child's physical, emotional, and social growth. This results in an out-of-balance person.

SPLINTERED SKILL. An isolated skill which is not an integral part of development. A skill which is not transferable to other learnings, which cannot be used to build on. For instance, a child who is not developmentally ready to draw a triangle can be taught to do this by connecting dots. However, the child will not be able to transfer this learning to either painting or execution of the letter A. This is skill usually acquired by *training* as opposed to learning.

THE DEVELOPMENTAL POINT OF VIEW

It is highly unlikely that anyone without a Developmental Point of View can really take part in a successful Readiness Program. This is not a program for those who feel that a child is like a piece of clay which can be pushed and pulled to fit a pre-determined form. Nor is it a program for those who feel that a child is like a computer for which information is broken up into little pieces and fed in bit by bit, to be retrieved at a later date. It is a program for those who have faith in the orderliness of nature and who trust children to know their own needs.

The Developmental Point of View means understanding that growth is orderly, structured, predictable. Because children are living organisms, they are subject to the same laws of growth as every other species in nature and have a cycle of development peculiar to humans in general. In this way each child is like every other child.

>*Children walk before they run.*
>*They think concretely before abstractly.*

The Developmental Point of View means respecting the fact that all children have their own rates and patterns of growth peculiar to them. In this way each child is different from every other child.

>*Children learn to walk at different ages.*
>*Some toe in, some toe out.*
>*Who dares to legislate the age children shall*
>   *walk, or which is better,*
>*Toeing in or toeing out.*

The Developmental Point of View means accepting children as total action systems; their physical, social, emotional, and intellectual components depending upon and supporting each other. These components are not separate, and one cannot be stretched ahead of the others without upsetting an intrinsic and intricate balance.

>*Children instinctively tend to seek balance necessary*
>*for their time and space at any given moment.*

1

The Developmental Point of View means appreciating that readiness for any given task has its roots in the biological-maturational make-up of the child. We can neither *produce it, hurry it, nor ignore it.* When children are ready, they will
> *be born*
>> *walk*
>>> *talk*
>>>> *read*

The Developmental Point of View means promoting educational programs for children in terms of development as it *is, now,* not in terms of what one thinks it ought to be.

The Developmental Point of View means walking hand in hand with nature. It is a respect for the total humanness of children.

THE OVERPLACED CHILD

Joey's fifth grade teacher asked the guidance counselor to find out why such a smart boy did such odd things. "He does only the top row of his arithmetic paper. He gets them all right, but it takes him all day. He simply can't bring himself to start anything—always asking me to repeat the directions just once more."

Joey's mother said, "Joey was born in December. The September before he was five, we sent him to kindergarten, which he hated. He wanted to go the first day, but after that it was a struggle every morning. The teacher told us he was young and immature, but we wanted him to have this opportunity, so we made him attend all year. Then when he was five and a half years old, he started first grade. The teacher told us he was young and immature, but that she was used to that. His father said, 'He's got to grow up sometime!' "

"We lived a mile and a half from the bus stop," the mother went on, "and Joey ran every step of the way home each afternoon, crying all the time."

School records showed that Joey was taken out of school in December because of a prolonged illness and reentered first grade the following September. Although his second try at first grade seemed very successful, there was a distinct decline in achievement with each succeeding grade. Family history indicated Joey to be a happy, well adjusted, and healthy boy until entrance to kindergarten.

As the counselor administered an interview-type test, she noticed that Joey watched her face very intently, overanxious about her reactions to him and to his answers. He could not bring himself to say "I don't know."

Piecing things together, the counselor now understood what had happened to Joey. His first introduction to school had taught him that mistakes and failures are unacceptable. They make people frown or yell or laugh at you. For the first year and a half of Joey's schooling, he had been put in a situation where he could do little except fail. He developed an anxiety about failure

3

which increases and reinforces itself each year. He trusted himself to do only one row of arithmetic, laboriously checking and rechecking each example. He just couldn't start another row because he might make a mistake! Joey's anxiety possesses him. It rules his every move. So that he can survive, he has put himself in a protective box and is pulling the lid down tighter every year. He cannot reach out to new things—to learning. Thus, in the attempt to give Joey an early start, the opposite has happened and his chances of becoming educated have been shut off altogether.

Children who go to school before they are mature enough to cope might suffer the rest of their lives for this one mistake in timing.

Although the law dictates that children must be in school by the age of six, it is impossible to legislate when they are *ready* for school just as it would be impossible to legislate when they shall erupt their first teeth or take their first steps. There is a great deal of variation among children regarding the time when they are ready for school. A sizeable number of them are not ready to cope with the school day at age six, and some are not ready even by age seven.

Legislation of this sort often causes us to take perfectly normal children into school too soon and thus spoil their chances of becoming educated. Unready children are trapped in a situation where they are humiliated in front of their friends every day, and survival becomes a matter of escape by daydreaming or clowning to solicit acceptance by peers; or when this is not enough, avoiding school as much as possible by developing psychosomatic illnesses.

OVERPLACEMENT MEANS THE CHILDREN ARE IN OVER THEIR HEADS. Their grade level imposes pressures which inhibit their growth in some area. It can inhibit social growth, physical well being, emotional stability, or academic learning. Wherever there is undue pressure, something has to give.

AN OVERPLACED CHILD IS FRUSTRATED. This frustration can be manifested covertly or overtly. Most children's

4

frustrations are a combination of both. It is common and easy for the educator to overlook covert frustration. It is easy to recognize overt frustration, but common for educators to consider it a matter of discipline rather than one of overplacement.

COVERT MANIFESTATIONS OF FRUSTRATION can take the form of avoidance, conformity, passive resistance, or overdrive.

AVOIDANCE is exemplified by the withdrawn child who stays on the periphery, escapes in daydreams, doesn't challenge, and demands nothing.

CONFORMITY might be the only defense possible for the overplaced child who uses most energies to learn the correct answers (this is so easy in the traditional, stimulus-response kind of education) but seldom succumbs to natural curiosity, to do some in-depth probing. The child slides easily into the routine of the prescribed school practices and keeps reasonably comfortable by the approval gained. This child seldom uses high level thought processes such as induction and deduction or synthesis and analysis. The mind is usually a vast wasteland of unexplored territory. Superficial goals are high report card marks rather than personal inner growth. Very bright girls often use this defense when overplaced.

PASSIVE RESISTANCE is a quiet way of handling undue pressure. "I don't care, so nothing can really hurt me." These children are spectators, not doers. They do not allow themselves to become interested in anything. They do what is comfortable to do. They don't argue. When questioned, or challenged, they do the expedient thing and agree. They passively resist the prescribed school practices, but they do it pleasantly and quietly.

OVERDRIVE is the most deceptive of all the defense mechanisms. The child achieves academically (usually not creatively), is a social butterfly who gets elected, shows normal emotional patterns, and often is a sports hero. This is the person who "has everything." What could possibly be

5

wrong with that? Nothing, except that this child will likely burn out at a very early age. This burn-out or collapse might come at any age, but it usually occurs in college and takes the form of dropping out, or a complete breakdown, or suicide. The child did everything too fast, and too soon. A little extra time at the age of six would have given the chance to blossom from within—at a normal rate. Instead, school overplacement caused this child to step up growth and perform at a burn-out rate; inevitably, all too soon—the child was spent.

OVERT MANIFESTATIONS OF FRUSTRATION are well known to most educators. That they are caused by overplacement, however, is not as well known. Most often, these symptoms are attributed to emotional disturbance, learning disability, or lack of discipline. This is not wholly inaccurate, since the behaviors described below usually are a direct result of emotional or learning problems. The emotional and learning problems, however, are in many cases caused initially by the child's starting school too early.

PHYSICAL REACTIONS to overplacement show themselves as fatigue, tenseness, and sometimes faulty perception. These children might be chronically absent from school, often with colds. They are tired much of the time and sometimes fall asleep at their desks. They are frequently seen with scowling, tense faces, with straining, squinting eyes. Parents sometimes report that these children collapse at home after school, both physically and emotionally. This is manifested by tantrums, frustration, crying, or napping. Strain on overplaced children can cause unreliable perception. They might appear deaf at times because they will hear only as much as they can absorb. Their visual perception can be inaccurate and inconsistent, seeming fine one day and poor the next.

SOCIAL REACTIONS to overplacement are indicated by children feeling uncomfortable with peers and uncertain about themselves. They have few, if any, friends. They quite often can relate better to children younger than themselves and frequently these children cannot relate honestly to anyone because their own ego development is so impaired.

These are the children who are not confident in group athletic situations. They often lash out with anger at their peers on the playground. Those who do not show anger usually go to the other extreme and withdraw into themselves and are sometimes labeled "loners."

EMOTIONAL REACTIONS to overplacement are rooted in feelings of inadequacy. These children feel unworthy, unwanted and unneeded in the world. They lack the confidence to do most things. They are easily brought to tears and display tensional outlets such as bed wetting, nail biting, and daydreaming. They are typically overanxious about physical contact on the playground and about always "being right." In the classroom, these children are restless, frequently sharpening pencils, visiting the nurse, going to the bathroom, and generally trying to escape the work at hand. The overplaced child is often an "angel" at school and a "devil" at home, or vice versa.

INTELLECTUAL OR ACADEMIC REACTIONS to overplacement are probably the easiest to discern. These children often have difficulty in finishing their work. Also, they might be erratic in achievement—doing well for one week and poorly for the next two weeks. High or average intelligence can be accompanied by low academic achievement and we hear the teacher say these things:

"John could do it if he would only *try*."
"Mary is an underachiever."
"Bill knows how to do it, but he just won't."

AN OVERPLACED CHILD MIGHT SUCCEED ACADEMICALLY. Some children, when put into school before they are ready, handle the situation by allowing their intellects to develop at a faster rate than other aspects of their beings. Because our society smiles fondly on intellectual children, they soon learn to put the major part of their energies into intellectual growth at the expense of physical, emotional, or social growth. Because they are in over their heads, something has to give.

OVERPLACEMENT USUALLY RESULTS IN SKEWED DE-

VELOPMENT. This means that one or two areas of the child's development grow at a faster rate than other areas of development. With each passing year, the gap grows wider until a distorted, one-sided, limited personality has developed. Children who enter school before they are developmentally ready cannot cope with the environment and they are forced to simplify their relationships to it and deal with it in a few areas only. Thus, they might become scholarly bookworms who don't join the team, learn to dance, relate to the opposite sex, or expand their social horizons in any way. Or, they might be the sort of children who put the major portion of their energies into developing social skills. They might become very empathic, likeable kids who use their popularity to cover up inadequacies in other areas.

THE POINT IS — WHEN WE FORCE
CHILDREN INTO SITUATIONS FOR
WHICH THEY ARE NOT READY,
WE INHIBIT THEIR CHANCES OF
BECOMING THE WHOLE PERSONS
THEY WERE MEANT TO BE.

MEET FOUR TYPICALLY OVERPLACED FIRST GRADERS

BRILLIANT BRUCE

BIG BILL

EXAMINER'S
RECOMMENDATION
Needs an extra year.
Although he's already reading
(taught himself at four) and intellectually superior, he's functioning in all other aspects like
a five year old. Placement in
first grade may result in skewed
development. A "superior
immature" who needs protection.

CLASSROOM BEHAVIOR
DECEMBER REPORT
Achieving A's
Spends all his time on academics
Has only one friend
Afraid of other children
Avoids playground and lunch-
  room
Anxious about physical
  contact

EXAMINER'S
RECOMMENDATION
Needs two extra years.
Although large physically, his
coordination is that of a four
year old, like the rest of his
behavior. Far from ready for
academics; may be labeled a
"slow learner" even though
mental development is on a par
with his social, emotional and
physical being.

CLASSROOM BEHAVIOR
DECEMBER REPORT
Failing
Academics irrelevant to his
  needs
Plays all day
Everlastingly good natured
Loved by everyone
In his own happy world

9

PUSHY PETULA

AVERAGE ALFRED

EXAMINER'S
RECOMMENDATION
Needs 6 months to a year.
Although bright and capable,
she is an extremely tense child
who pushes herself. Needs the
dividend of extra time so she
can achieve easily, without
strain.

CLASSROOM BEHAVIOR
DECEMBER REPORT
Achieving well academically
Pushes herself to be best in
  everything
Anxious that she might do
  something wrong
No friends
Tense—cries often
Chronic nasal infection
High absenteeism

EXAMINER'S
RECOMMENDATION
Needs 6 months to a year.
December birthday. Development is in keeping with his age,
but too young for prescribed
first grade. A well-balanced
child who feels good about himself and his world; he might sacrifice
that confidence trying to keep up
with children a year older.

CLASSROOM BEHAVIOR
DECEMBER REPORT
Slipping in academics as
  complexity increases
Sullen at times
Beginning to disrupt the class
Enjoys the reaction of his class-
  mates when he's disruptive

THE ASSESSMENT OF SCHOOL READINESS

WHY EXAMINE? Using chronological age as the criterion for entrance into standardized school situations presumes that all children develop at the same rate. However, there is a two-year range in the readiness levels of a group of normal six-year-olds. An assessment of the children will determine each child's degree of readiness to handle the situation (usually kindergarten or first grade) and a school placement can then be made according to the child's readiness to sustain emotionally, socially, physically, as well as intellectually in that situation.

WHO SHOULD DO THE EXAMINING? Anyone who has had developmental training, who trusts both children's feelings and his or her own feelings about children, and who has a high regard for total human growth—not simply academic achievement. The examiner might be a teacher (of any grade level), the guidance counselor, the school nurse, the reading specialist, or even someone brought in from the outside. The examiner must be intelligent and have the perseverance to pursue training and continuous study in child development as it relates to school readiness.

WHEN SHOULD THE EXAMINING BE DONE? The best time to examine seems to be in the spring previous to school entrance. If this is not feasible, then as early as possible in the summer. This gives time for the parents and children to adjust to any changes in plans and to prepare for the child's placement.

The question is often asked, "Isn't this too early? Won't the children develop in the remaining months?" The children will develop some, but there are rarely great spurts, and the examiner keeps this in mind when making projections for the fall. Results of spring testing have proved accurate for fall placement.

WHERE SHOULD THE EXAMINING TAKE PLACE? In a quiet, pleasant room in the school that the child will be attending. Large systems that provide a central "clinic" where hundreds of children are examined in a short time are apt to have difficulty because of the impersonal "cold" atmosphere. Parents must feel that *their* school, *their* principal, and *their*

11

staff care about *their* child.

WHAT EXAMINATION SHOULD BE USED? At this time the most comprehensive examination available seems to be the Gesell Developmental Examination. It provides a way of looking at children as they are *now,* finding out where they are on the growth continuum. The examiner gives the child specific tasks to do and observes not only how they are handled, but also behavior, body stance, level of speech, concepts, sustaining power, and emotional outlets. Since this is an attempt to look at the children as they really are, there are no wrong answers on a developmental examination. Each child performs correctly according to his or her development at this time.

SOME ADVANTAGES OF THE GESELL DEVELOPMENTAL EXAMINATION

It is a placement tool, not primarily a diagnostic tool.

It is a tool that allows the examiner to look at a child as a total action system and to be as concerned about the child's emotional needs as the intellectual needs.

It is personal. Children enjoy the experience. Most of them feel very special and very smart afterward. This thirty minutes of undivided attention is very uplifting to children.

The training necessary to learn to become an examiner provides some very valuable side effects. There is usually a marked change of attitude in the examiners. They look at children entirely differently from the way they did before and become much more aware, more child-centered teachers. Their approaches to teaching might change drastically. Many examiners start to grow personally and become very valuable agents of change in the school system.

SOME DISADVANTAGES OF THE GESELL DEVELOPMENTAL EXAMINATION AS COMPARED TO OTHER SCREENING TOOLS

It cannot be self-taught. One must go through a period of intensive training to be able to administer and evaluate the exam.

Since it is administered individually to each child it is time consuming. A full developmental examination takes approximately thirty minutes to administer and as long again to evaluate. Most examiners using a full battery find they can handle only four or five examinations a day. A short developmental examination (usually called a screening) takes fifteen to twenty minutes to administer and as long again to evaluate. Using the short form, an examiner can do eight or ten a day.

Because the exam is largely based on observation of the child by a trained examiner, it is more difficult to score than the usual, numerically averaged, objective tests.

It is difficult to explain to parents and staff since they are used to thinking of readiness in terms of what a child knows or can do rather than where the child is functioning on the growth continuum.

WAYS TO GET TRAINING IN THE GESELL DEVELOPMENTAL EXAMINATION

The Gesell Institute conducts workshops to train examiners both at the Institute and in other areas of the country upon request. In some states, individuals who have had extensive training and who have worked with the exam over a long period of time are now training other examiners. These people may be located by contacting State Departments of Education, local Teacher Training Colleges, or the Gesell Institute.

Anyone interested in training should contact:

The Gesell Institute of Child Development
310 Prospect Street
New Haven, Connecticut 06511

Tel: (203) 777-3481

ARE OTHER TESTS AVAILABLE?

Because of the disadvantages of the Gesell Developmental Examination, a school might want to look for another instrument. This is not recommended, except in an emergency situation, because that school would not gain what are perhaps the most important facets of Gesell training—the developmental point of view, knowledge of child development, and a change of attitude on the part of teachers.

Many school readiness tests are being developed because of the interest in readiness at the present time. An examination of several of these, however, reveals that most of them are not child development oriented, but tend to emphasize intelligence or skill development—which leaves out many important aspects of the child's growth, such as the ability to cope and to sustain.

Other examinations might be successfully used for screening of incoming children if administered by an examiner who has had training in the Gesell Developmental Exam and who transfers the learnings.

CHARACTERISTICS OF A GOOD READINESS ASSESSMENT

It is individual.

It takes into consideration the social, emotional, and physical development of the child as well as the intellectual.

It is largely based on observation of the child by a skilled examiner who has thorough knowledge of developmental sequences.

It is administered by someone who has had special training in child development.

SOME ADDITIONAL THOUGHTS

Additional information about the child is very important

and should be included when possible; physical, optometric, and auditory examination, information from the parent interview, as well as observations and recommendations of the pre-school teacher.

A nursery or kindergarten teacher *with the developmental point of view and thorough knowledge of the growth continuum* (and who is not skills oriented) can often make as good a prediction as the exam.

One successful, economical way to use the Gesell Developmental Exam is to use the short form (screening) on all the Pre-First-Graders. The long form then needs to be used only in cases where the evaluation of the short form is questionable.

PLACEMENT ALTERNATIVES

PRE-KINDERGARTEN EXAMINING

The best time to do a developmental examination is before kindergarten entrance.

Prevention of over-placement at that time can save much difficulty for both the child and the school system later on. Many private kindergartens are happy to cooperate with the public school. The more adjustments that are made at the kindergarten level, the fewer later on.

If pre-kindergarten children are examined, there will be three groups of children: 1) those who are ready, 2) those who need one-half to one year of extra growth time, and 3) a few who need one-and-a-half to two years of extra growth time. Placement for each of these groups is different, but correct placement or adjustment at the kindergarten level can mean that most will be ready for grade one when they enter. There might be one or two atypical children for whom placement will be difficult and who need special consideration.

THE READY CHILD who enters kindergarten is usually ready for first grade the following year.

CHILDREN WHO NEED AN EXTRA YEAR may get this time in a number of ways. The main thing is that they *get* this extra year. They will enter first grade at age seven. They may:

Spend two years in kindergarten.

Be asked to stay home a year and come to kindergarten the next year.

Be placed in kindergarten with the understanding that they will be placed in the Pre-First-Grade room the following year.

17

CHILDREN WHO NEED TWO YEARS (there are always a few) need special consideration. They do need two years, and facing this in the beginning can save a lot of trouble later on. They will enter first grade at age eight. They may:

Be asked to stay home a year, attend kindergarten the following year, and then be placed in a Pre-First-Grade room.

Attend kindergarten for two years and then be placed in a Pre-First-Grade room the following year.

Stay home for two years, then enter kindergarten the next year.

PRE-FIRST-GRADE EXAMINING

The school that doesn't have a kindergarten program and has been unable to make adjustments at that level will not have as many alternatives for placement, but there *are* alternatives.

Again, if the children are examined before first grade there will be three groups: 1) ready children, 2) those children who need an extra year, and 3) those children who need two years.

THE READY CHILD will go to first grade and is usually ready for second grade the following year.

THE CHILD WHO NEEDS AN EXTRA YEAR may be:

Asked to stay home or go to a private kindergarten for a year. (If both the school and parent agree, there is usually no difficulty.)

Placed in a Pre-First-Grade room and then go to first grade the next year at age seven.

THE CHILD WHO NEEDS TWO YEARS may be:

Asked to stay home a year, be placed in the Pre-First-

Grade room the following year, and go to first grade at age eight.

Placed in a Pre-First-Grade room with the understanding that two years will be spent in that room. Some schools have two Pre-First-Grade rooms and a child needing two years spends a year in one, and then moves on to the next.

SOME ALTERNATIVES WITHIN SCHOOLS

In setting up a readiness program, school administrators must examine facilities and resources very carefully to see just what alternatives are available. They must also project their plans two or three years hence to see what this will mean in terms of space and teacher needs. It is cruel to give children a Pre-First-Grade experience and then move them into second grade because of a space problem. The administrator must always keep in mind that *nothing* can substitute for that extra year; GROWTH MUST HAVE ITS TIME.

Because of cramped facilities, administrators often make use of a combination of alternatives. They might arrange with some parents to keep their children home or have these children repeat kindergarten. They might place others in a Pre-First-Grade room. Some parents prefer to keep their children home a year, while others will demand entrance. In most cases, setting up a readiness program will take much creative and courageous thought on the part of the administration.

SOME TYPICAL SCHOOL ARRANGEMENTS

This is not an attempt to exhaust all the possibilities but to suggest some of the more typical arrangements schools make to provide a Pre-First-Grade experience for their unready children.

THE SCHOOL WITH ONE FIRST GRADE and no kindergarten perhaps has the most difficulty in setting up a program, because this might entail combining two grades. If the second grade is small, the best combination would be the second graders with the ready first graders in one room, and the Pre-First-Grade children in the other. It is much easier for a teacher to handle two grades when the children are ready to settle down to work than one grade when half of them need a movement-experience program.

There is of course the possibility of a Pre-First/first combination with a different set of expectations for each group. This is a difficult set-up for a teacher to handle and an aide should be considered a "must." One special problem with this combination is that it is difficult to protect children from pressuring themselves, and if they do this and meet with academic success, it is hard to give them the extra time they need. A school faced with the difficulty of the Pre-First/first combination might explore the possibility of half day attendance for each group. Neither the Pre-First nor the first grade children are really ready for a full day.

THE SCHOOL WITH TWO FIRST GRADES has the facilities to begin a good readiness program. In this case, one first grade becomes a Pre-First room, and the other remains a first grade. It is recommended there be no more than twenty children in the Pre-First-Grade room; fifteen to eighteen seems to be ideal.

THE SCHOOL WITH THREE FIRST GRADES usually arranges facilities so that there is a Pre-First-Grade, a combination Pre-First/first (or borderline) group, and a first grade. With this set-up, the children in the borderline group are often shortchanged. Many of them need a young program and extra time, and very often they get neither. It would be more realistic (if one looked at the children realistically) to have two Pre-First-Grade groups, and one first. The tendency has been to cater to the ready children, believing they are the norm and setting up standards for six-year-olds which only the most mature can handle well, causing the borderline children to be pushed.

KINDERGARTEN AS IT RELATES
TO THE READINESS PROGRAM

KINDERGARTEN DOES MANY WONDERFUL THINGS FOR CHILDREN. In guiding five-year-olds through their development, it provides rich, exciting experiences, provides an opportunity for social interaction, and makes a fine bridge from home to school. *The one thing it cannot do, however, is hasten maturation.* So, no matter how excellent the kindergarten program, if one is thinking in developmental-maturational terms, there will still be only one-half of the children ready for first grade at the end of the kindergarten year.

IN SOME COMMUNITIES, KINDERGARTEN IS THOUGHT OF AS A SORT OF "PREP SCHOOL" FOR FIRST GRADE. Head Start, also, has been considered as a "getting ready for." This kind of thinking is unfortunate, because the importance of time is overlooked, and such a kindergarten produces the same kind of pressuring situation now prevalent in most first grades.

KINDERGARTEN MAY TAKE THE PLACE OF A PRE-FIRST-GRADE ROOM in a community if it admits only those children who are developmentally ready, thus compensating for the developmental-maturational factor. Or it may take the place of a Pre-First-Grade room if it keeps half of the children in kindergarten an extra year.

THE PRE-FIRST-GRADE ROOM, HOWEVER, DOES NOT TAKE THE PLACE OF KINDERGARTEN in that the Pre-First-Grade room does not provide an educational experience for children who are chronologically five years old.

THE MAIN DIFFERENCES IN THE KINDERGARTEN AND PRE-FIRST-GRADE ROOM ARE: 1) children in the kindergarten are usually chronologically five years old, and 2) those in the Pre-First-Grade are six years old.

THE TWO PROGRAMS ARE VERY SIMILAR and should be so if one keeps in mind that the children in the Pre-First-Grade room are five or five-and-a-half in development. This does not mean, however, that the children repeat the same program. The kindergarten and Pre-First-Grade are both materials-centered, experience oriented programs. The children use all the materials in different ways. Their performances are not repeated. Kindergartners who plant seeds might do it again in the Pre-First-Grade room the following year, but they will broaden their experiments by providing different kinds of growing environments for their plants—same children—same materials—but a more sophisticated approach.

THE KINDERGARTEN CAN MAKE A GREAT CONTRIBUTION TO A READINESS PROGRAM. The kindergarten is a good place to observe the children and to identify, over a period of time, those children who are unready. This observation, added to the examination, helps many parents accept the idea of added time.

THE KINDERGARTEN TEACHER should not be intimidated by the first grade teacher who wants the children to know their numerals and letters before coming to first grade. The kindergarten teacher, perhaps better than any other teacher, sees children as they really are. The teacher should feel, and be, free to fulfill their developmental needs as they are now, and not be concerned about getting them ready for next year.

A POINT OF VIEW ON DISABILITIES

It is the opinion of the authors that while there *are* children with inherent learning disabilities, many of the children thus labeled are the victims of overplacement who *become* disabled. Correct initial placement for entering children should be a first priority and lead to fewer children labeled "learning disabled."

DISABILITIES FALL ROUGHLY INTO THREE CATEGORIES, those of a physical nature—deafness, blindness, etc., those of an emotional nature, and those defined as "learning" disabilities.

OVERPLACEMENT CAUSES TENSENESS AND INHIBITION and because of this, overplacement might be the cause of any one of these disabilities. Children unconsciously inhibit their own intellectual, physical, neurological, social, or emotional growth when living with constant frustration.

THERE ARE TWO VERY OLD AND VERY TIRED EXCUSES commonly used by educators when a child is not doing well in school.

1. The child suffers from emotional disturbance which is caused by home conditions—divorce, immorality, quarrelling, etc.

2. The child is victim of an inherent learning disability. A most popular learning disability at the moment is "dyslexia" with "minimal brain damage" running a close second as a status saver. One insightful guidance counselor recently stated, "This community is suffering from two epidemics. One of them is the flu and the other is dyslexia."

PERHAPS EDUCATORS SHOULD TAKE ANOTHER, LESS DEFENSIVE LOOK at disabilities. When they do, they might see that:

1. There are innumerable basic practices in most schools which contribute to poor emotional health, e.g., report cards, authoritarian teachers, crushing of creativeness

23

and individuality, public reprimand, standards of achievement unrealistic for many, etc.

2. Schools, because they are run by professionals, could be therapeutic, counteracting forces for children from unstable homes. School programs could be organized so as to fulfill the basic human emotional needs of achievement, security, acceptance, and affection. Schools could give priority to making each student feel worthy.

3. The symptoms of dyslexia, such as difficulty learning to read, reversals in reading and writing, hyperactivity, restlessness, inability to be accurate in details, inattention, particular difficulty in writing and spelling, clumsiness, forgetfulness, are also the symptoms of minimal brain damage, emotional disturbance, and *overplacement. Most children do not display these symptoms until they start school!*

SOME CHILD GUIDANCE CLINICS AND PSYCHIATRIC INSTITUTIONS make diagnoses by measuring the child against the prescribed, arbitrary standards used in school. In this light, many normal children appear abnormal.

PERHAPS IT IS TIME TO ASK OURSELVES:

1. Is the child disabled or is the school disabled?

2. Is the school crippling the child with its predetermined, arbitrary standards?

THE PRE-FIRST-GRADE ROOM—
AN ENVIRONMENT FOR LEARNING

Children who are six years old expect to go to school, ready or not. Actually, many of them are not ready, and for these children, a Pre-First-Grade experience is recommended.

The Pre-First-Grade room is an environment for learning for those children who are six years old chronologically, but who are five or five-and-a-half in development and who need extra growing time. It may be called by another name but essentially has three main characteristics: 1) the children are six years old and eligible for first grade by law, 2) the program is movement-experience oriented, and 3) most of the children will go into first grade the following year.

GOALS OF THE PRE-FIRST-GRADE ROOM

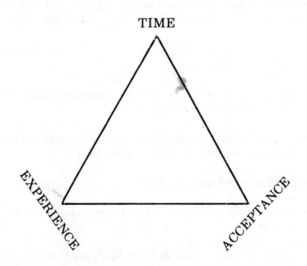

The Pre-First-Grade room exists to provide children with:

TIME to grow and develop as nature intended them to. There is no pushing or attempt to "get them ready," but a respect for nature's timing and the patience to let each child's

25

readiness emerge.

EXPERIENCES through which they can make discoveries about things, about life, about themselves—experiences requiring involvement of the whole child.

ACCEPTANCE without condition; respect for the unique human being each is; and trust in each child's goodness and capabilities.

OBJECTIVES OF THE PRE-FIRST-GRADE ROOM

To give the child time to grow.

To help develop a strong sense of self—to allow each child to "blossom from within."

To provide an environment rich in equipment and materials, where experiences are direct and concrete, to build the foundation for later, more abstract experiences.

To provide movement experiences for development of physical and motor skills.

To promote growth in visual, auditory, and tactual perception—to sharpen the senses.

To provide an opportunity to learn and practice patterning of all kinds—visual, auditory, kinesthetic.

To provide listening activities.

To provide many and varied opportunities for oral expression.

To build a foundation for sophisticated math concepts through manipulation of concrete materials.

To build a foundation for chemistry, physics and biology, through discovery and play with blocks, and natural materials such as water and sand.

To help the child relate to others socially and be a part of a group.

To help the child develop problem-solving techniques.

To promote creative expression through art, dance, music, cooking, story telling.

To help the child develop the habit of success.

To help the child establish an environment of beauty, order, and stability.

SOME BASIC IDEAS WHICH WILL FACILITATE AN ENVIRONMENT FOR LEARNING

MOVEMENT IS INTENSE COMMUNICATION. There should be freedom of movement throughout the day as well as some times set aside for exercise of the large muscles and exploration of space. All learning is based upon movement. Children who have control of their bodies have control of the world.

SOCIAL INTERACTION IS A WAY OF LEARNING ABOUT ONESELF AND OTHERS. Basic to a sense of self is a knowledge of oneself in relation to others. Learning takes place much more rapidly when there is communication—a sharing of ideas and experiences. Children should be free to interact, and equipment—telephone, walkie-talkies, puppets, etc.—should be provided for those children who find communication difficult.

PROBLEM SOLVING IS A WAY OF CONTROLLING THE ENVIRONMENT TO ENHANCE ONE'S NATURAL DEVELOPMENT. Children who have not developed this skill are at the mercy of anyone wishing to manipulate them—they have no power. Children learn to solve their own problems through social interaction, through taking responsibility for their own decisions, and through manipulating such materials as blocks, water, and sand.

DISCOVERY OF SCIENTIFIC PRINCIPLES,

MATHEMATICAL LAWS AND RELATIONSHIPS IS EXCITING TO YOUNG CHILDREN. It fosters a joy and eagerness for learning. This discovery takes place when materials are provided for exploration—not when the teacher is looking for answers. When children are "told" an answer, they are cheated out of many chances of discovering or creating an answer within themselves.

CREATIVITY THROUGH ART, MUSIC, DANCE, AND COOKING, PROVIDES AN OUTLET FOR INDIVIDUALITY—a way of sharing oneself with others. There should be opportunities daily for each child to experiment with a creative medium. Following a model should be discouraged, although children do get ideas from others and this should be accepted as a natural way of learning.

LANGUAGE DEVELOPMENT IN THE YOUNG CHILD IS ORAL. When children are ready for reading, they will read—but only what they can speak; and they can only speak about that which is in their experience. Again, they must come into contact with all kinds of experiences which they can explore, assimilate and talk about.

THE SENSES—SEEING, HEARING, SMELLING, TASTING, AND FEELING—ARE THE PATHWAYS TO KNOWLEDGE. Children need all kinds of opportunities to sharpen these senses and talk about what they perceive.

REALNESS DEVELOPS AS ONE GAINS A SENSE OF SELF AND THE FREEDOM "TO BE." It comes from knowing "I like myself," "I am worthwhile," "I am needed," "I have good ideas." It is the key to happiness and is fostered by teachers who are themselves real and who value the children as individual beings—capable of making decisions for themselves which will foster their own development.

FACTS ARE IMPORTANT ONLY AS THEY MEET THE CHILDREN'S NEEDS TO SOLVE A PROBLEM, OR ARE A MATTER OF INTEREST TO THEM. They will remember only what is meaningful to them.

SKILLS LEAD TO COMPETENCY, A FEELING OF BEING

INDEPENDENT. But skills without basic knowledge and understanding are meaningless.

Development of skills should take place only as the child needs them. There is no sense in teaching grammatical rules to a child who has never written an original sentence. Nor is there any need to teach computational skills to a child who doesn't understand the meaning of number. Teaching skills before a child is ready for them can be not only useless but outright damaging—especially if the teaching causes the child to shut off—to block out future endeavors. Children whose small muscle development is still immature can be harmed by having to copy letters and numerals before they can adequately hold a pencil. Children who are still making vertical and hortizontal reversals can be harmed if reading is forced on them—perhaps becoming future "dyslexics."

A rule of thumb about skills development—if the child needs the skill, asks for it, *appears ready* for it, give it. If there is any doubt—*wait.* The child who is really ready will attempt it unaided.

It is quite possible to teach or train children *before* they are developmentally ready. Because *they can be taught,* we are fooled into thinking they are ready.

THE PRE-FIRST-GRADE ROOM HAS NO CURRICULUM (course of study). There is no skills continuum. Skills are learned as they are needed to solve real problems.

THE ENVIRONMENT, RATHER THAN THE CHILDREN OR THE PROGRAM, IS STRUCTURED. The room is usually set up in activity centers with abundant materials in each center for the child to explore and manipulate. These centers are not for the children to go to after they have completed their work—these centers *are* their work.

EMPHASIS IS ON LEARNING, NOT ON TEACHING. The children cue the teacher, who helps them move in their own individual directions—to explore those activities which interest each one. The teacher has no preconceived idea of what the child must learn or the order in which this

29

learning must take place.

THERE ARE GROUP ACTIVITIES AS WELL AS individual activities. Teacher and children work together to become a "family" with concern for one another. Group meetings are held frequently, and rules established when needed.

ROUTINES AND RITUALS ARE ESTABLISHED TO PROVIDE SECURITY, but are flexible enough for each child to adjust, and few enough so that creativity isn't stifled.

THE ENVIRONMENT IS ORGANIZED so that each child knows the use and place of each piece of equipment. The children are responsible for keeping materials in order and for tidying up the room. Enough material is displayed to encourage exploration, but not so much as to cause confusion. Displayed material is changed often.

EVERY CHILD IS VALUED as a unique human being, and because the child is valued, so is the child's work valued. Teacher and child work together to make something the child is proud of, thus leading to pride of self. Beauty is also valued, and teacher and children work together to make the room a beautiful place in which to live.

TEACHING IN THE PRE-FIRST-GRADE ROOM IS AN ART. The learning that takes place depends upon the creativity, humanness, and knowledge of child development on the part of the teacher and the interests and needs of the children. Not all teachers are comfortable in such an open environment.

SOME SPECIFIC IDEAS WHICH WILL FACILITATE AN ENVIRONMENT FOR LEARNING

COOPERATIVE STRUCTURING OF THE ROOM. The children and teacher should set up the room together so that the environment truly belongs to them all. This in itself becomes a learning experience. The room should change throughout the year to meet new needs.

FLEXIBLE RECESS TIME. The out-of-doors should be as

much a part of the classroom as the indoors. A creative teacher might want to spend a whole day outside, or might want to have simultaneous activities going on inside and outside. Some rooms with an outside door have a fenced-in area which becomes an integral part of the classroom. Even if the children go out only for a specified time each day, the classroom teacher is the best one to judge when they need this.

SPONTANEOUS REST. A tired child needs to rest, and might curl up in a corner or under a table. Some rooms provide a cot where the child may rest. Although specified rest times are helpful for most, they should not preclude consideration for the child with individual needs.

FREEDOM TO GO TO THE BATHROOM. Going to the bathroom is not a privilege but a necessity. Children should be free to go without question. Having to ask has caused many embarrassing moments. Many children want privacy and won't use the facilities unless privacy is assured.

ENCOURAGING INTERACTION. Silence is not only unnatural—it inhibits development and learning. Language development comes through speaking, and learning is reinforced through social interaction.

ELIMINATING GRADING. If a child is accepted as a unique individual,with a unique rate and pattern of growth as well as individual interests and inner drive, and if one truly respects individual learning, then grading is a sham—a destroyer of integrity—both the child's and the teacher's. Conferences with parents a couple of times a year are much more meaningful and helpful to the child.

RESPECTING INDIVIDUAL ORAL EXPRESSION. If the teacher interrupts to correct oral language, the child might soon stop speaking. The child can be helped to use good language by the teacher's use of it—thus providing a model.

ELIMINATING NEGATIVE CORRECTION MARKS. Mistakes are a way of learning—they suggest lack of understanding—or the need for an alternate way of looking

31

at the problem. A cross mark is a final indictment, a value judgment that does nothing to help the child to look for an alternate method of solution. Better to emphasize the positive and help correct the negative.

SUGGESTIONS FOR EQUIPPING A PRE-FIRST-GRADE ROOM

Two lists are included in this section; one for a fairly substantial budget and one for a very small budget. It is expected that each teacher will be creative in adapting these suggestions to the particular school, community and budget.

In general it is best to buy good quality only, because inefficient equipment frustrates children and breakage hurts them.

It is best to display only a few items at a time since too many stimulating objects are confusing to the child.

The out-of-doors is an invaluable classroom. Nature walks, field trips and excursions enrich the program greatly. The surrounding community can be brought into the classroom, also. Police, musicians, artists, and hobbyists might be invited to bring their special equipment to demonstrate to the children.

Sometimes the High School Shop department can be involved in making part of the equipment. The High School sewing class might make puppets or bean bags. Parents also like to be involved in making equipment.

It is particularly important for the children that good care and good storage of equipment be provided. Puzzles and construct sets might be stored in plastic or wooden boxes. Spray cardboard boxes with plastic mist to give them strength and longer life.

BLOCK AREA

Construct sets

It is unwise to cut expenses in the Block Area—one of the most important activity centers—by buying inferior blocks. Instead, buy fewer blocks, precision-made of hard wood. Basic principles of engineering and construction are being formed by this activity. Fundamental concepts in relationships of size, weight, area, and seriation are formulated. Habits of order, cooperation, control, economy, initiative, perseverance, and concentration are fostered by block play.

Open shelving is desirable for storage because standards of order are developed when the child places, and then *sees* largest blocks neatly placed, next largest beside them, etc. Block carts which encourage the child to toss in blocks, helter-skelter, tend to contribute to an unordered, chaotic state of mind.

So that children do not become discouraged by running out of pieces when their structure is half finished, large construct sets are important.

SCIENCE AREA

Expensive	*Inexpensive*

Sand table
  sifter, containers
Water play table
  turkey baster (squeeze bulb),
  cake decorator (plunger),
  plastic tubing, funnels,
  sprayer, etc.
10 desk-top magnetism labs
2 tuning forks
Stethoscope
Rope and pulley set
Electrical invention box
Giant magnifier
6 single magnifying glasses
Jumbo hourglass
Pan balance scale
Adjustable fulcrum balance
Gerbils and cage
Aquarium and equipment
Terrarium
Bolt-tight
	Make a sand table by setting a water
	  play tray on two desks
	Plastic baby bath for water play
	Two bar magnets
	Iron filings
	Tuning fork
	Stethoscope
	Two magnifying glasses
	Egg timer (hourglass)
	Pan balance can be made with peg
	  board, paper clips, and aluminum
	  pie plates
	Fulcrum balance can be made from a
	  variety of ordinary things
	Empty gallon mayonnaise jars from
	  the cafeteria, or gallon paste jars
	  from the art dept. make good
	  aquariums (tadpoles) and terrariums
	A box of junk machinery may be do-
	  nated by parents—old clocks,
	  appliances, bathroom scales, radios,
	  —equip with various kinds and
	  sizes of screwdrivers

Science for the very young child is mostly involved with living things, the world around us.

The out-of-doors, in all seasons, furnishes a wealth of free material for scientific investigation.

"Telling" is apt to deprive the child of the best opportunity to learn. Unhurried, unstructured observations and experience allow the children to wonder and to draw conclusions which are appropriate for their particular levels of thinking. Rather than instructing, the teacher facilitates learning by furnishing an abundance of manipulative materials for experimentation and by arranging opportunities for various new experiences.

MATH AREA

<table>
<tr><td>Expensive</td><td>Inexpensive</td></tr>
</table>

Expensive	*Inexpensive*

Giant dominoes
Number sorter
Peg boards
Wooden pegs (2 boxes)
Giant counting rods
Stepping-stones
10 counting frames (abaci)
Judgments & Readiness
    (10 complete desk-top labs,
    basic geometric forms,
    judgments of "less or
    greater" set theory)
Aluminum liquid-measures set
Three dimensional parquetry
Jumbo additive blocks and board
Fractional circles board
Fractional squares board
Fruit plate (fractions)
	Most of the manipulative materials
	    can be made by parents, teachers, or
	    high school students, using pictures
	    in various equipment catalogs as a
	    guide. Laminated, corrugated card-
	    board can be used to make giant
	    dominoes, footsteps, stepping-
	    stones, etc.
	Concepts of number, size, weight, etc.
	    are learned from other equipment
	    in the room such as blocks, water,
	    and sand
	A few simple math games may be
	    purchased

Verbalization of basic number relationships is what is important; paper and pencil work lends little to the intellectualization of math concepts. The writing of numerals is apt to be an inhibiting force. Also, rote counting is of little value. Counting *things,* however, is a learning experience.

When playing "store," use real money; play money contributes to a visual distortion.

LANGUAGE AREA

Expensive	*Inexpensive*

Tape recorder and cassettes
Play phones and walkie-talkies
Puppet theatre and puppets
4 sets of Early Childhood
    Discovery Materials
    (MacMillan Co.)
Lotto games
Puzzles for visual discrimination
	Play phones and walkie-talkies
	1 set of Early Childhood
	    Discovery Materials
	    (MacMillan Co.)
	Lotto games (some might be made
	    by teacher)
	Puzzles for visual discrimination
	    (some might be brought from home)

A puppet theatre could be made of a cardboard box. Puppets made by parents.

Language for the Pre-First-Grader is oral. It is important to remember that *reading* and *writing* are built on a foundation of *listening* and *speaking*. Visual, written symbols are a representation of auditory, spoken symbols.

The development of language in a child is the same as the evolution of language in humanity. Babies' first involvements with language are listening. After a year or so, they imitate sounds they have heard and they speak. Several years later, when suitable neurological growth has occurred and when there is a felt need to record, they start to transpose the auditory symbols into visual (written) symbols.

Children can learn to read and write

only to the extent that they can listen and speak.

Time spent on the fundamental areas of language (listening and speaking) is the best way to help the child learn to read and write well.

Very simply, then, the teacher's role seems to be to provide:

Things to talk about and

opportunity to talk about them.

Everything that happens in or out of the classroom furnishes things to talk about. Each new experience provides new vocabulary and new patterns of speech.

The assimilation of these new words and speech patterns takes place through discussion, casual conversation, puppetry, creative dramatics, and other forms of group interaction.

LIBRARY

Expensive	Inexpensive
Two rockers	Entire stock may be donated by families whose children have outgrown the books.
Folding book rack	
150 books	
	Have a book fair in cooperation with a book company. Parents come and buy a book to donate to the library.
	A local service organization might be happy to furnish the library as their year's project.
	A library table might be made of old school desks.

It is wise to buy books with library binding. Well-kept books enhance the delight of the library area. Remove damaged books. Parents can help with book repair.

Take pains to include some of the classics, e.g., *Little Red Riding Hood, Three Bears, Mother Goose.*

Encourage children to lend some of their favorites to the library. Enthusiasm is catching.

Put out a few books at a time and change them often.

Children like to make their own picture books to add to the library.

The purpose of books in the Pre-First-Grade room is to foster interest in books, to allow children to discover that delightful stories come from books and that many happy hours can be spent with books. Pre-First-Grade children should be encouraged to read the pictures in books, but not the words.

ART AREA

Two aluminum double easels
30 x 60 table
Drying rack
Scissors
Brushes (2 large)

Expendable Materials
Finger paint paper (5 pkgs)
Finger paint (3 qts of each—
blue, green, red, yellow)
Newsprint for brush painting
(9 reams)
Tempera (1 gal. each—white,
black, red, blue, yellow) Other
colors are made by mixing
primary colors
Potter's clay—200 lbs.
Colored construction paper
(24 pkgs)
Paste (1 gal.)
Chalk and crayons

Inexpensive

To make an easel, glue two wooden
blocks on seat of old school chair and
lean the pad of newsprint against
the chair back.

Push together four old desks to make
a work table.

String nylon cord along one wall to
hang pictures to dry.
Brushes (3 large)
Scissors

Expendable Materials
Some money may be saved by using
old newspapers instead of newsprint.
Glazed shelf paper makes good finger
paint paper.
Household materials may be used to
make paste, finger paints, and clay.
Some potter's clay should be used,
however, some of the time.

The idea here is to encourage the children to *express* themselves through materials. If they like their products, they are good and should be displayed.

In creative endeavors, the *process* is very important to the child's development and the *product* is very important to self-esteem.

Place the art area next to the sink.

Provide a box of *beautiful junque* donated by parents—feathers, discarded jewelry, ribbon, cloth swatches, empty spools, etc.

Soft chalk is better for creative expression than crayons. Encourage the children to use the *side* of the chalk or the *side* of large crayons.

Furnish left-handed scissors when needed.

The more *body* involvement, the better (finger painting, clay modeling, etc.)

Basic to the art area are: lots of tempera paint and large brushes, lots of finger paint and good potter's clay.

Avoid these inhibiting factors: patterns, models, demonstration, coloring books, duplicated papers, water colors (too small), 9 x 12 paper for painting, a "too neat" area.

MUSIC AREA

Expensive	*Inexpensive*
Record player for child use (good quality)	Use school record player. Have children bring records from home. Borrow records from town library.
25 - 30 records	
Autoharp	
Assorted rhythm instruments	Make rhythm instruments as a class project.
	Autoharp should be purchased.

The primary purpose of music is to provide enjoyment. Music is also a means of self-expression, a vehicle for enhancing one's self-concept, and a way of providing relief from tension.

Hopefully, the teacher will have some means of accompaniment—piano, guitar, or Autoharp. The Autoharp is suggested here because it is an easy instrument to master.

Child participation is as important as listening. They participate by singing, dancing, marching, or playing a rhythm instrument.

Records should include classics as well as simple children's pieces.

HOUSEKEEPING AREA

Expensive	*Inexpensive*
Heavy wooden sink with waterproof work surface, removable water tray	Have parents make a wooden sink, refrigerator, and stove. Or a dishpan on a table can serve as a sink.
Heavy wooden stove	
Heavy wooden refrigerator	Dress-up clothing can be donated—or
Heavy wooden cupboard	bought at a rummage sale for very
Doll bed	little
Stand-up mirror	Parents can donate furniture, dolls,
Tea set, utensils, etc.	teddys, etc., that their children no
Child's table & 2 chairs	longer use.
Doll buggy	Dishes, pans, etc., can be brought
Dress-up clothes (donated)	from home.
Trunk or chest of drawers	Minimum equipment to buy if not
2-6 dolls (include 2 washable	donated: Stand-up mirror
rubber babies)	Child's table & 2 chairs
Rocking chair	Bureau
Housekeeping set	
2 telephones	
Wooden doll house	
Doll house furniture	

An important part of the young child's developing process of symbolization is the playing of roles. Children who are five or five-and-one-half, developmentally, identify with home and family, so it is quite natural for them to assume the roles of mothers and fathers. Boys enjoy this as much as girls.

The housekeeping unit fosters good social and emotional growth and makes a strong contribution to language and ego development.

WOODWORKING AREA

Expensive	*Inexpensive*
Workbench with vise	Workbench (made locally)
Tool board	or cut down discarded
4 claw hammers (assorted weights)	teacher's desk
2 sets screwdrivers	Pegboard for tools
1 chisel	2 claw hammers (assorted weights)

2 saws	1 screwdriver set
Small adjustable wrench	2 saws
2 vises	Vise
Miter box	1 hand drill & bits
2 pairs of pliers	Chisel set
Rulers - yardsticks	Wrench
Hand drill and bits	1 pair of pliers
6 lbs. nails (assorted sizes)	Miter box
include a box of roofing	6 lbs. nails & screws
nails - screws	(include roofing)
Sandpaper (assorted)	Assorted dowels
Dowel rods (assorted)	Sandpaper (assorted)
Soft wood and mill scraps-various	Ruler - yardstick
widths, lengths, and thicknesses,	*Soft* wood and mill scraps - various
from local lumber dealer	widths, lengths, and thicknesses,
	from local lumber dealer

Avoid toys or tools of poor quality. Children needs saws that saw and hammers that hammer. Girls enjoy this area as much as boys do.

Get a local carpenter or a parent to come in and explain how the tools are used and cared for.

Don't expect "finished" products.

Wood is a fine medium for creative work.

Place the workbench against a wall and wedge it between two tall cabinets so there is room for only two children to approach it at a time. This automatically reduces the dangers brought on by overcrowding. Because this activity is excessively noisy, a time limit might need to be set for wood-working.

BODY BALANCE

Expensive	*Inexpensive*
There is no limit to the amount of equipment that can be bought for the gym and for the out-of-doors. Long-range plans should provide for one large piece of equipment	Materials for walking beam and balance board (homemade)
	Make a portable hopscotch and twister game out of oilcloth

to be bought each year.

To keep in the room:
Balance board and walking
  beam
Wibbler (balancing device)
Tumbling mat
Portable hopscotch
Twister game
Crawling tunnel
Tin can stilts (homemade)

Fasten together large cartons
  for a crawling tunnel

Tin can stilts (homemade)

The younger the child, the more gross motor activities must be provided. The opportunity to move freely in large spaces is essential to normal development of the human organism. The inner sense of laterality and directionality which is a prerequisite to later discriminatory skills is developed only by bodily movement in space. It cannot be taught. Only the child's bodily movement can allow it to develop.

Intellectualization, including higher thought processes, has its basis in motor patterning.

MISCELLANEOUS EQUIPMENT

Expensive

Shelving units
Vacuum cleaner,
  broom, dustpan, mop
Eight trapozoidal tables
10 chairs (stacking)
Carpeting for half the room
  (not in sink, art, water play,
  or animal areas).

Inexpensive

Shelving made from planks and
  cinder blocks
Vacuum cleaner (rebuilt),
  broom, dustpan, mop
Make table with a sheet of plywood
  set on old desks or on sawhorses
10 chairs (stacking)
Salvage old 9 x 12 rugs from families.
  If they are worn or skimpy, fasten
  them to floor with wide plastic tape.

One whole wall of shelving built in is cheaper and more efficient than separate units. It is poor economy to purchase materials and then not provide adequate storage space.

Each child should have an individual "cubby" in which to keep personal belongings. A polaroid picture of the child tacked to the cubby will mean a lot.

42

Every effort should be made to deal with noise in the Pre-First-Grade room, short of inhibiting the children from talking and moving about. It isn't the noise itself which is disturbing, but the reverberation of that noise off hard surfaces in the room. Energy expended (and it is considerable) tolerating the noise would be better spent in pursuit of effective ways of controlling the noise. Some things which absorb sound are carpeting, acoustical ceilings, unpainted concrete block walls, and drapes. Devise all possible means to cover hard surfaces with soft material. Room management also offers some help toward controlling sound:

> Extend classroom to include out-of-doors (more space per child).
> Limit (by arrangement) woodworking to two children at a time.
> Arrange noisy areas behind tall room dividers.
> Make sure block play takes place on carpeting.

It should be noted that the Pre-First-Grade program suggested here does not include paper and pencil (reading and writing) work. It is the opinion of the authors that denying paper and pencil activities at this level does not in any way hold children back, or slow their learning opportunities. Rather, it is felt that it protects them from many of the ills of a too-early introduction to this very sophisticated stage of human development. Children at the Pre-First-Grade level have not yet acquired the neurological maturation necessary for success in use of the written symbol which is the last intellectual skill developed in the evolution of humanity. Certainly, Pre-First-Grade children could be *trained* to use the written symbol, but it would serve no useful purpose at this time in their lives and would leave the door open for the development of confusing visual reversal patterns, feelings of inadequacy and other symptoms generally referred to as *dyslexia*.

Very high level intellectualization goes on in the manipulation of sand, water, blocks, and all the other materials proposed for the Pre-First-Grade room. The written symbol is but a representation of that

43

intellectualization and can better wait until sufficient neurological maturation takes place.

Wanna
see our
room?

Wanna
know what
we do?

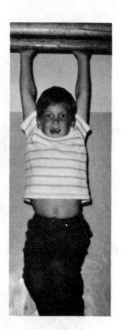

Well look!

Here it is ———>

We're lucky;
we get to move around all the time.

My teacher says,
         "If your body moves well,
          so will your mind,"

But we have rules —
we make them up ourselves, like
          ...no running in the room
          ...take care of stuff
          ...don't bother other kids.

We've got a walking board to do exercises on, tin can stilts,
      Johnny Jump Up, and a
      Twister game.

We go to the big gym
      where
      we run and skip,
      turn somersaults,
      and dance.

On our playground we have
      a tunnel to crawl
      through, a ladder to
      climb on, a rail to
      balance on, and a
      great big swing
      made out of tires.

We roll, and crawl, and climb; and run fast and jump high
      ...but only when we're supposed to.

We're luckier than the other kids — they sit still almost
      all day long, but not us...

         We can grow

         We can learn

              BECAUSE WE MOVE!

It's important that our bodies help our brains to think
and solve problems.
...So we have a block and puzzle area.
It's on the RUG because sometimes...

BLOCKS

ARE

NOISY

We've got...lots of great big blocks, lots of little blocks
...leggos...toggles...and tinker toys.
We've got stuff to help our eyes to see better,
And stuff to help our hands do very careful work...
So that we can build better and
better things,
And solve harder and harder problems...
Because when we're big,
We'll have to solve important
problems

And we'll have to solve them

ALONE

We're going to be good readers and writers because we do lots of
things like...listen to stories on the tape recorder...or make
up stories...any stories we want. I can operate the tape
recorder all by myself.

I look at the books in our library, and I know what the story's
about even before my teacher reads it. We have lots of
books, new ones all the time. Some of them don't have any
words, and you can guess what they say.

We can make our own books. We draw the pictures and tell our
teacher what it says and she writes it down. We put our
books in the library for the other kids to read. I like these
books best.

We have puppet shows and
plays.

We talk on the telephones
and the walkie-talkies.

Some days some older kids
come to read to us and we
talk about stories and act
them out.
I already learned a word
all by myself.
I'll tell it,
but I won't write it
    YET!
Do you know why?

ИНOℲ

We do lots of *number work*.
We *count* everything...books, straws, shoes, and even each other.
We *measure* everything...with ribbon, sticks, or hands
   to find out what's smallest or even who has the biggest feet.
We *weigh* everything...blocks, pumpkins, even guinea pigs.

We...
      fill bottles and spoons and cups with sand —
      sometimes dry sand,
      sometimes wet sand.
      play store with real money,
      make grids and matrices,
      play checkers and dominoes.

We jump on the number ladder,
And play leap frog and musical chairs, counting up and down.
We solve very important problems, sometimes together and
   sometimes alone.
        We look for different ways to figure things out.

Do you know that the numbers never, never end? I do!
You can just go on...and on...and on!

We have a science corner where we discover just about
everything.
    We plant seeds and bulbs,
    Look at things under the magnifier,
    Hatch guppies in our aquarium,
    Float things in our water table,
        and
    Make mazes for our mice.

Some days we taste things and talk about sweet, or sour, or
bitter.
    And we talk about soft and hard, or gooey or crunchy.
We watch and listen and feel things.
    Sometimes we smell them or
    taste them to discover all we can.

Lots of days we go outdoors
    to draw our shadows
        on the playground,
    Or look for crawly things
        in the pond,
    Or find different kinds of leaves.

One day we collected sap
    to make maple sugar,
    and once,
    we saw a dam some beavers made.

To discover things, you have to look —
    very carefully,
    and listen, and smell, and touch —
    very carefully.
    You have to think about things —
    sometimes a long, long time.
    You have to ask yourself questions —
    sometimes a lot of questions
    And sometimes a lot of people a lot of questions.

                                                  BUT...

When you see something new, and listen to it, or touch it,
or taste it,
and think and think and think
and ask and ask and ask,

you DISCOVER IT,

AND THEN YOU KNOW.......FOREVER.

Today in our art area
   I made a clay elephant. My teacher knows someone who has
      a kiln, and she's going to cook my elephant to make
      it hard.
   Some other kids made a big picture. They cut out stuff and
      pasted it on and my teacher hung it in the hall.
   We've got four big painting easels with big brushes and
      bright paint in big jars. We can paint anything we want.
   We cut and paste, and finger paint. We can make
      everything.
   We've got...

buttons and ribbon

plastic bottles and
   scraps of leather

and feathers for
   Indian hats

and plaster of paris
   to make prints.
      We've got...

lots and lots of clay

and egg boxes

and styrofoam and
   yarn.

   And one day a lady came and we all learned to weave cloth.
   We make a big mess. But my teacher doesn't care because
      we know how to clean up after we're finished.
   Our room is decorated with all the beautiful things we've
      made.
   If we don't make a mess sometimes, our room wouldn't be
      pretty and we wouldn't know how to make nice things.
         And that would be...
            Very very sad...
               Because no one would know what kind
               of people
               WE ARE!

We're very important people. In our room we can be anyone...
a mommy or a baby,
an airplane pilot,
a garage man,
a dancing lady,
a big bear,
a fireman.
Sometimes we like to dress
up and look at ourselves
in a big mirror.
We talk to each other all
day long, and play
together and
work together.

I am needed in
this room...
to make pretty
things to hang...
to talk to Janie
when she's
lonesome...
to help my teacher
keep track of
things. I feel
good when people
need me.

Sometimes our teacher smiles
and laughs out loud.
Sometimes she get mad,
and sometimes she cries,
But that's all right,

        WE
            DO

                TOO!

I like to look at a smily face.
It feels good when you smile.
My friends like to see me smile.
I have lots of friends.

Sometimes I wonder about ME. I wonder what I am like.
I wonder
    if I am like Bill,
    or Jean, or Matthew.
I wonder what I will be
    when I grow up.
I wonder how it feels to
    be good, to be bad,
    to be a baby,
    to be grown up.

I wonder if the other
    kids wonder about
    ME.

My teacher said
    she wonders too.

CHARACTERISTICS OF A PRE-FIRST-GRADE ROOM

The ratio of pupils to teacher is not more than 20 to 1.

Equipment and materials are placed so that children have easy access to them.

Rather than individual desks and chairs, there are activity centers for small group work; science area, math area, library, block corner, etc.

Bulletin boards are used to display child-made things, not teacher-made things.

There is a sand table in the room.

There are large blocks suitable for building forts, houses, and so forth.

There is an abundance of manipulative materials.

There is an art area with easels, drying racks, and other related materials.

There is an opportunity for water play nearly every day.

Books are one of a kind for teacher reading and children browsing.

At least 30 minutes each day (other than recess) are given over to gross motor activity.

There is at least one cooperative planning session a day between the teacher and the children.

Rest for each child each day is encouraged.

At least one half of the time is given over to individual rather than group learning experience.

There is opportunity to be alone if the child chooses.

A child who is unhappy or bored with an activity is allowed to go on to something else.

Children who are absorbed in an activity are usually allowed to continue for as long as they wish.

Children move about and talk and help one another without permission.

Work with letters and numerals is de-emphasized.

Rather than duplicated papers, creative work is encouraged.

Frustration and stress, as evidenced in the posture and on the faces of the children, is minimal.

COMMON MISCONCEPTIONS ABOUT THE
READINESS PROGRAM

THAT SCHOOL READINESS IS READINESS TO LEARN OR READINESS TO READ. School readiness is the ability to learn and to cope with the school environment without undue stress, and to *sustain* this level of learning and coping. Many children who are ready to read are still not ready for the school situation. They might manage the academics, but usually at great expense to another part of their being—social, emotional, or physical. They might actually turn off real learning and compensate by rote learning or memorizing.

THAT INTELLIGENCE MUST BE CONSIDERED BEFORE OTHER ASPECTS OF GROWTH. This misconception is somewhat related to the former. However, it must be stressed that one does not use intelligence in isolation. No matter how intelligent children are, they cannot use their capabilities to the fullest if they have no friends, are physically ill, or are emotionally in trouble. In fact, stress in any area can impede learning, and prolonged stress has the effect of reducing intelligence. Children are a total action system, and their potentials are activated only by the smooth functioning of the whole system.

THAT SCHOOL SUCCESS IS ACADEMIC SUCCESS. School success might better be defined as learning academics and having enough energy left over to live a well-rounded life. Thus many "straight A" students may be considered school failures because they've never developed the forces necessary to cope with the environment in self-enhancing ways. They shun personal contacts, sports, have fewer creative outlets, and in general live rather narrow lives.

THAT READINESS MUST BE IMMEDIATELY NURTURED. There need be no worry that if readiness occurs and is not instantly fed it will disappear forever. Readiness only becomes stronger with time, and in fact can become so strong that children will teach themselves.

THAT A PRE-FIRST-GRADE ROOM IS A PLACE TO "GET" CHILDREN READY FOR FIRST GRADE. There is no attempt

57

to "get" children ready in this room; in fact there is no evidence that there *is* any way to "get" them ready. In the Pre-First-Grade room, readiness is allowed to *emerge* as nature intended it to. There is a respect for nature's timing. An experiential environment is provided; both for enhancing or enriching growth, and for providing a foundation on which future, more abstract learnings can be built.

THAT THE PRE-FIRST-GRADE ROOM IS A PLACE FOR SLOW LEARNERS. Many so-called "slow" children are really smart *young* children. If the readiness program is handled well, some of the brightest children in the school will be in the Pre-First-Grade room.

THAT UNREADY CHILDREN ARE ABNORMAL. There can be as much as two years difference in the maturity of *normal* children at the same chronological age. Approximately half of the entering first graders are not ready for that situation, and these children are perfectly normal.

THAT THE READINESS PROGRAM IS A "HOLDING BACK." The readiness program actually allows a gift of time and the privilege of moving in a forward direction. When children are put in a situation they can't handle, they're immobilized. What might seem to be a "holding back" will actually allow them to move ahead.

THAT CHILDREN "CATCH UP." This has been an age-old hope of parents and teachers of slower-maturing children, but most of these children never do "catch up." Some might seem to (the late bloomer!) but they usually do this at the expense of some aspect of their beings, or by using compensating techniques—learning to "play the game."

THAT THE PARENTS ARE TO BLAME IF THEIR CHILD IS UNREADY. Considering the deluge of written material being circulated today advising parents that they can raise a superior child by intellectual stimulation, the push toward early reading, and the current television shows purporting to produce readiness, it is no wonder that parents feel responsible and guilty if their child is not ready. *No one is to blame.* The best of parents, the best of environments, still produce children who need growing time. Parents need educating to the concepts of school readiness and reassurance on this point.

THAT THE READINESS PROGRAM IS A FORM OF NON-GRADING. In actuality, it adds another grade—before first grade.

THAT IF A SCHOOL IS NON-GRADED, THERE IS NO NEED FOR A READINESS PROGRAM. This *might* be true *if* the school provides for children's developmental needs, not simply their academic needs; *if* the program is materials and experience oriented, rather than skills oriented; and *if* the non-grading extends through high school and *children can absorb time when they need it.* A non-graded school which makes placement a matter of achievement, and which is geared to a progression of skill learnings, *does* need a readiness program.

THAT THE READINESS PROGRAM IS A PANACEA. It's *not,* but if handled well, it can help alleviate many future school problems for a great many children, teachers, and parents.

COMMON MISTAKES THAT SCHOOLS MAKE RELATIVE TO THE READINESS PROGRAM

FORGETTING THE PARENTS—not fully educating them *before* the child is examined—not involving them in the growth of the program—not meeting with them personally to explain the child's placement.

NOT INCLUDING THE JANITOR AND THE LUNCHROOM PERSONNEL in staff orientation. Lack of information often opens the way for misinformation to start circulating.

NOT BEING WHOLLY COMMITTED TO THE CONCEPT, or being afraid of confrontation—sneaking the program in through the back door. This creates a lack of trust in education and educators. Parents have a right to know how their taxes are being spent.

HAVING PARENTS MEETINGS BEFORE THE PRINCIPAL OR SPEAKER IS FULLY INFORMED—fully committed—*very* knowledgeable. Parents want straight, honest answers. If they give their support, they want to know that all aspects have been explored, and the administrator is fully committed to carrying out a successful program. They want to know what will happen next year and the year after.

GOING TOO FAST. Deciding in May to have a readiness program the following September, leaving no time to work through a strategy.

HAVING NO ONE PERSON IN CHARGE for coordinating the program—checking on strategy, working with principal, examiner and teacher, to make sure all are doing their parts, each knows what the other is doing, and they are all working together. This is especially important in a city where many schools are involved, or if private kindergartens are cooperating with the public schools.

NOT ENOUGH "PERSON TO PERSON" CONTACT IN THE CITIES. Having all children examined in a central clinic and sending out a dittoed statement concerning placement. Parents in cities need more contact with their schools than people in small towns. Because of bigness they feel more manipulated—more helpless. By having children examined in neighborhood schools with person to person contact, much of this dissent could be minimized.

USING A SKILLS-ORIENTED TOOL (such as reading readiness tests, I.Q. tests, or even a checklist of isolated developmental skills) to identify those children who need a Pre-First-Grade experience.

LETTING THE PRE-FIRST-GRADE ROOM BECOME A CLASS FOR SLOW LEARNERS, atypical children, disadvantaged children, or children with disabilities — a "catch-all."

PUTTING CHILDREN FROM THE PRE-FIRST-GRADE INTO SECOND GRADE the following year.

HAVING A "WATERED DOWN" FIRST GRADE CURRICULUM IN THE PRE-FIRST-GRADE room with the addition of some "readiness" activities. The program suggested in this manual *is* the program, not an addition to the program.

PROVIDING PRE-FIRST-GRADE ROOMS FOR LESS THAN HALF of the entering children. For instance, having one Pre-First-Grade room and three first grades. That's not enough; there should be two of each.

BEING SWAYED BY THE ACADEMIC ACHIEVEMENT of the "superior immatures," thus overplacing them.

ADMITTING UNREADY CHILDREN TO KINDERGARTEN knowing they might not get the extra time they need. A dedicated teacher often wants to accept these children, knowing that they can be given a happy year, but forgetting that they are being set up for twelve years of over-placement.

SAYING, "WE DON'T NEED A READINESS PROGRAM, WE'RE GOING TO INDIVIDUALIZE." Individualization, while a very necessary and commendable change, does not solve the readiness problem. It usually provides a flexibility in terms of academics only.

A STRATEGY FOR CHANGE

Establishing a Readiness Program involves more than an acceptance of the philosophy and a desire to initiate such a program. Two main requisites are: a real commitment and a well-thought-out strategy for change. The following strategy, based on five years of successes and failures, is offered as a good model for educators to follow in initiating a Readiness Program.

> *Change involves accepting people as they now are, emotionally and intellectually, and transferring them gently, gradually, and patiently to another emotional and intellectual phase.*

SOME GENERALITIES ABOUT CHANGE

THE STATUS QUO is a very strong force. Innovators have to prove that the change is good. No one has to prove the status quo is good. It stands on its own merits, even when it has none.

INTELLECTUALIZATION WITHOUT EMOTIONAL IN-VOLVEMENT will not bring about meaningful or lasting change. Instead there will be a lot of lip-service which is not translated into actual behavior modification.

SOME DISSENSION WILL INEVITABLY EXIST. A goal of 100% of the population becoming avid supporters of the change will only bring disappointment. Aim for a realistic percentage.

STRESS IS A CONSTANT INGREDIENT of change. This is true even when the change is wanted and is agreeable. Stress means there is a certain amount of instability experienced by the participants of the change.

ONE CHIEF REASON FOR FAILURE in attempting to bring about change is the lack of a well-thought-out, planned sequence of events preceding the change.

A FIRM COMMITMENT is required for change to take place.

INVOLVEMENT OF THE ENTIRE COMMUNITY is necessary for lasting school changes.

AUTHORITARIAN COMMAND does not bring about healthy or lasting change.

SUGGESTED STRATEGY FOR IMPLEMENTING A READINESS PROGRAM

SIX STEPS

1. Educate STAFF ....January
2. Educate PARENTS ....January
3. Train EXAMINERS ....February, April
4. Examine CHILDREN ....April, June
5. Decide on PLACEMENT ....June
6. Interview PARENTS ....June

STEP ONE—EDUCATE STAFF

A unified staff is reassuring to the community, especially at a time when innovation is taking place. Harmony can be achieved only if all personnel focus in on the same understandings.

Small groups should be arranged so that the participants will feel free to talk and question in each other's presence. (Lunchroom personnel might be inhibited in a group of teachers.)

All school personnel should be included—custodians, bus drivers, lunchroom helpers, volunteers, aides, supervisors—anyone who works in the school and with the children.

All the concepts presented to the parents as well as some particular ones for educators should be discussed. (See THE AVERAGE PARENTS NEED TO LEARN, pg. 87, and THE STAFF NEEDS TO LEARN, pg. 71.)

"Where the educator is now" requires tactful presentation at these meetings. (See SOME

STUMBLING BLOCKS FOR EDUCATORS, pg. 75 .)

STEP TWO—EDUCATE PARENTS

This step is the foundation upon which the whole change will be built. If it is not successfully executed, discontinue efforts to make a change. If taken seriously and carefully planned, however, this step can be a most exciting and satisfying experience.

Experience has shown that the parent is less threatened by this change in school entrance policy than the educator. Most parents easily take to the idea of walking hand-in-hand with nature.

Meet in small groups of 10 to 15 parents at a time. People tend to be silent in large groups. Self-expression, questioning, and discussion are essential if learning is to take place. Coffee klatches or evening meetings in various homes make an inviting atmosphere.

Profit from the enthusiasm of parents who are already convinced, who have had children benefit from a readiness program either in the local school or in another community. Use these parents as speakers, as panel members, or discussion leaders.

An outside expert might be useful as chief speaker (an expert is a person away from home, of course). Have the concepts presented by a principal, examiner, or Pre-First-Grade teacher from another town in the state.

All parents of incoming first graders should attend these meetings. If necessary, hunt them down in the home to get them to listen; but they must be educated at this time.

Parent education must be repeated every year for several years.

The speaker should start out with an understanding of "where the parents are now" and then carefully plan a

65

presentation of the concepts needed. (See THE AVERAGE PARENTS NEED TO LEARN, pg. 87.)

Filmstrips, movies, and other visual aids say more than a thousand words. (See Bibliography.)

A printed pamphlet for parents to take home is helpful. Include a brief summary of pertinent information. Make it attractive, easy to read; have it professionally printed if possible. Athena Publications has a parent pamphlet available.

Publication of a series of articles on child development and school readiness in the local shopper or newspaper is a good way to disseminate information as a prelude to parent meetings. These should be written by a local person, knowledgeable about school readiness, and should be short, to the point, and written from a human interest (rather than local news) point of view. Present one idea or topic in each article.

STEP THREE—TRAIN EXAMINER

A developmental assessment of each child at school entrance will reveal a developmental or functioning age. This, rather than chronological age, will be used to indicate placement of the child. Because this is a very sophisticated procedure based on an in-depth knowledge of child development, a Developmental Examiner must be trained.

Any vitally interested person might acquire this training—principal, teacher, supervisor, nurse, counselor.

Learning to "read child behavior" takes a strong commitment because many hours of hard study and practice are required.

Whichever exam is used, the examiner should have the specialized training in child development which makes for a knowledgeable, subjective evaluation of the exam.

(See THE ASSESSMENT OF SCHOOL READINESS, pg. 11 .)

STEP FOUR—EXAMINE CHILDREN

All incoming kindergartners or first graders (or both) need to be given an individual exam.

The cut-off date of each community is best adhered to. Very few chronologically young children are ever found ready. It isn't worth the trouble to do special examining of those who are six after the cut-off date. The extra time can only strengthen these children, even if they are ready.

A pleasant introduction to school for both the parent and child may occur at the time of examining. This is a good time for them to meet the principal and teachers, and to see the rooms.

While the parents wait for the child to be examined, they might read a pamphlet on school readiness, listen to an information tape, or watch a film presentation. This is a good information-gathering time for the parents.

The examiner needs to guard against the trap the parent inadvertently sets; "How did my child do?" A casual answer to this question might need to be retracted later. Careful evaluation of the exam and grouping with the principal need to be done before this information is ready for the parent.

A definite (and early) date should be set when the parent will be given the results of the exam. The parent needs this assurance before leaving the school.

If the parents are denied the chance to watch the examining, they might feel suspicious, uneasy, insecure.

If the parents are invited to watch the examining, they might become defensive about certain specifics of the exam because they can't possibly understand the evaluation of it. Also, they might misunderstand the examiner's enthusiastic acceptance of all the child does, thinking it indicates that the child is ready for first grade.

An examiner can do four or five full battery exams a day, or eight or ten screening (pre-kindergarten).

Attempts to use a group screening test first, and then administer Developmental Exams only to the questionable ones have been unsuccessful. The important developmental characteristics are not observable in the group test, and wrong judgments of a large number of children will be made. This process almost invariably does an injustice to the superior-immatures, the intellectual, achieving children who need more time to grow from within in *all* their total humanness.

STEP FIVE—DECIDE ON PLACEMENT

After all the examining has been completed, the examiner and principal work out the grouping.

Giving the children the benefit of the doubt means giving them extra time rather than pushing them on a little too soon. Remember that a child is not hurt by waiting, but irreparable harm might result from even a slight degree of overplacement.

The child's needs should be the only factor in considering placement. Space, time, etc., can be worked out in some way, but nothing can substitute for the extra growing time some children will need.

About 50% of the incoming first graders (based on many years of examining experience) will be developmentally too young for entrance to first grade.

Although placement is a cooperative effort, ultimate responsibility for each child's placement must remain with the principal.

STEP SIX — INTERVIEW PARENTS

(See THE PARENT INTERVIEW, pg. 94 .)

EDUCATION OF SCHOOL PERSONNEL

THE STAFF NEEDS TO LEARN

ALL THE ITEMS LISTED under THE AVERAGE PARENTS NEED TO LEARN, pg. 87 .

OVERPLACEMENT is a far more serious condition than might appear on the surface. They need to know the definition of overplacement and the symptoms of it. They especially need to learn that overplacement is often *not* manifested by academic failure.

SCHOOL SUCCESS is much more than academic success. Success must encompass the total child, not just intellectual growth. Many academically successful pupils are school failures, for they are achieving at the expense of their social, emotional, and physical growth.

SCHOOL READINESS is far more than readiness to learn. It is readiness to learn *in the school situation* without undue stress. Most children are ready to learn (on their own terms) before they are developmentally ready to go to school profitably.

READING READINESS is *not* school readiness. Many children who are ready to read, and who indicate this by reading readiness tests, will not be able to learn to read *in the school setting* because they are not developmentally ready to *cope* with that strenuous environment.

ABILITY IS NOT MEASURED by I.Q. tests, but rather by consideration of the functioning level of the whole child. Intelligence is not enough without the social, emotional, and physical development to support it. Actually, children's abilities are best measured by "what they are doing now"; how they are functioning. People tend, like water, to seek their own level. It is natural to reach out, in an accepting and stimulating atmosphere, for that which one *can* accomplish.

REMEDIAL STUDENTS are made by the school. No one

71

enters school as a remedial student. If accepted *where they are on the developmental continuum,* children will be placed in situations which are conducive to their growth as persons and they cannot become remedial students. However, if they are measured against the arbitrary standards (grades) which most educational programs are based upon, they have a great chance of becoming remedial students. Examples of such arbitrary standards are: grade placement by chronological age, report cards, standardized achievement and I.Q. tests. The students *are* what they *are* and they can't change that. The arbitrary standards are the only things which can be changed, and they should be changed to prevent the creation of remedial students.

MANY ASPECTS OF HUMAN DEVELOPMENT are *nature-ordained,* and thus cannot be influenced by environment.

IT IS PERFECTLY NORMAL for all children to become ready for school, but they will do it in *their own time,* at *their own rates of growth*; some might not be ready before age seven or eight.

REWARDS FOR ALL EDUCATORS ARE MANY

Classes tend to be made up of "ready" children; more capable, eager, and independent. This makes the teachers' job more pleasant and productive. Very little of their energies are spent on keeping order; they can devote their efforts to education.

Classes in which the majority of students are autonomous and independent produce a climate rich for experimentation with innovative ideas.

There is a decrease in discipline and emotional problems. When children are ready, they are interested in their educational pursuits and do not develop the behavioral traits which are born of frustration, boredom, and poor self-image.

There are few "poor" report card marks. Developmentally ready children are eager for learning and are usually capable students. Thus, the old ideas of grading on a normal curve become obsolete.

"End-of-the-year" confrontations with parents are reduced markedly. There are very few retentions because most children who start off at the right developmental level are able to maintain the educational lock-step with no trouble.

Therapists and remedial teachers will no longer be "a drop in the bucket," but might conceivably be able to take care of all or most of the needy students.

Many of the difficulties which are unique to the Junior High years will be eliminated.

The number of high school dropouts will be reduced.

There will be less waste of the taxpayer's dollar, since reducing the incidence of failure results in more education obtained for each dollar spent.

ROLE OF THE EDUCATOR IN THE READINESS PROGRAM

PRINCIPAL

Becoming educated to the concepts underlying a readiness program constitutes the principal's prime duty. This can best be done by taking a course in School Readiness and Developmental Examining. Even though the principal plans to do none of the examining, he or she needs to thoroughly understand the concepts involved. Study of this manual, reference to books in the bibliography and observation of operating readiness programs in other schools will also add to this understanding.

The strategy for change is the responsibility of the principal, who is the one who plans the strategic steps to be taken in the best sequence to bring about this change (see section A STRATEGY FOR CHANGE, pg. 63). The principal arranges for the parent orientation meetings and might be the chief speaker; plans the staff orientation meetings and assumes the leadership at these gatherings; and sees that someone becomes trained as a developmental examiner. Although the examiner recommends placement of each child, the principal is responsible for decisions made. The principal may carry out the individual conferences with parents, sometimes in conjunction with the examiner, after the exams are finished.

The equipment for the Pre-First-Grade room is purchased by the principal, who works with the teacher to choose it and then, since much of it is heavy and must be manipulated, sees that the teacher has help in placing it in the room.

Evaluation of the readiness program is done at the end of each year (see section EVALUATION OF THE READINESS PROGRAM, pg.101).

Dissemination of the results of this evaluation is the responsibility of the principal, who sees that the community is informed each year. The principal also makes this information available to the staff members and to other schools.

DEVELOPMENTAL EXAMINER

Continuous study of the developmental concepts underlying the evaluation of the exam is a duty of the developmental examiner. There is always more to learn and the examiner would be well advised to make periodic checks of evaluations by talking them over with other examiners.

Becoming well educated to the whole area of School Readiness is important for the examiner, who, more than anyone else except the principal, will carry responsibility for its success. Knowing how to assess the child's readiness is only *part* of the picture.

Examining the pre-schoolers is, of course, the main

function of the developmental examiner.

Making recommendations for placement of each child to the principal according to the results of the Developmental Exam is the examiner's responsibility.

Informing parents of exam results may be the responsibility of the examiner. However, this might better be done as an administrative duty or as a team effort.

Clear, concise reporting of exam results to the principal is the examiner's responsibility. Decisions made on those recommendations are *not* the examiner's responsibility, but are the responsibility of the principal and the parent.

Reeducation of the staff and community regarding child development and school readiness is an ongoing task for the examiner, one of the best-informed persons. Staff changes, and new families moving into the community, make this a continuing obligation.

OTHER SCHOOL PERSONNEL

Everyone who works for the school—bus drivers, superintendent, supervisors, nurse, lunchroom helpers, custodians, teachers at all levels—has a supporting role to play in this change in education. They need to display faith in the concepts and do all they can to make the people of the community understand what is going on. In order to do this, they need to become informed by reading and by attending the meetings which the principal arranges.

SOME STUMBLING BLOCKS FOR EDUCATORS

Educators might find that certain preconceived beliefs and practices get in the way of their gaining an understanding of the developmental point of view.

THE SPLINTERED SKILL has long been a device by which

teachers have deceived themselves into thinking they were aiding the child's growth when they were actually inhibiting it. By laboring, by carefully-thought-out pedagogical steps, and by stimulus-response techniques, the educator has taught isolated skills which give immediate gratification, but which do not enhance total development and do not lead to the child's growth as an independent person. The child does, in fact, become an addict who is more and more dependent upon this teaching.

LETTING CHILDREN LEARN instead of making them learn might be very difficult for teachers who have spent years teaching and learning still more techniques of teaching. Many teachers will feel they are not earning their money if they are not writing lesson plans and standing in front of the class making presentations. Actually, *letting* children learn is a very fine art. It calls for an entirely new way of conducting a classroom and is very hard work.

FEAR OF PARENT DISAPPROVAL might loom as a big obstacle to such a change. It takes a lot of courage to embark on a course which has never been traveled before, in the face of possible opposition by those people who pay the salaries. However, experience has shown that parents are the easiest group of adults to educate to the developmental point of view, perhaps because it is a way of walking hand-in-hand with nature. Parents do this rather instinctively in bringing up their children.

OVEREMPHASIS ON INTELLIGENCE is perhaps the largest obstacle for the educator, all of whose training and work experience have emphasized the importance of increasing intelligence. Most textbooks and teaching materials are geared to pushing intellectual growth. It is often a long, hard journey for educators to reach the point where they really *know* that the brain is functional only to the extent it is *integrated with social, emotional, and physical systems.*

ADMITTING NEED FOR CHANGE might be a hurdle. Change of any kind carries with it an unavoidable implication that what you have been doing all along has been wrong or unwise. This kind of admission to yourself might be hard, to say nothing of admitting it publicly. However, it is useless to think in terms of change until you can make this admission.

CERTAIN EDUCATORS MIGHT HAVE SPECIFIC BLOCKS

SUCCESSFUL TEACHERS often feel they have no reason to change. They are successful! Why should they rock a boat which has provided them with such a smooth journey! Change is very threatening to these people. Some of the most successful readiness programs, however, have been carried on the shoulders of Successful Teachers. They are so highly respected and trusted by the community that parents easily assume credence in whatever they say or do. They have a special effect on the staff, also, because if these successful people can admit there is need for change, then others should be able to also.

GUIDANCE COUNSELORS tend to look for abnormality rather than normality. They spend much of their time counseling children *after they are already in trouble.* Thus they are tuned in to "mopping up" operations rather than preventing problems from developing in the first place. They are apt to think of a child who is not ready for school at six years of age as abnormal or immature instead of simply developmentally young.

In addition, counselors might find it difficult to allow the developmental point of view to supersede their preconceived beliefs in the I.Q. and in achievement test scores.

Elementary Guidance Counselors, however, are in a unique position to aid in this preventive work and many counselors are rising to the challenge.

SCHOOL NURSES often have a particular orientation which causes them to think in terms of expedient remediation to keep things running smoothly—eyeglasses, vitamins, medicine, tutoring, rest. This tendency is strongly supported by the observable, immediate, positive results obtained, and tends to shut out thought of the need for long-range preventive measures. When children are given the time and conditions for natural development, the need for expedient remediation is greatly decreased. Actually, however, as educators go, nurses are among those who find it easier to understand the developmental point of view.

KINDERGARTEN TEACHERS have their own special set of problems which might interfere with embracing the developmental point of view. Financially, it might be hard to equip the kindergarten with materials which are developmentally appropriate for five-year-olds. Paper and pencils are cheap. What's more, paper and pencil work is expected and accepted by many parents and educators, so there is great temptation to stay with it. These forces can cause the kindergarten teacher to mentally reject the idea that work with the written symbol is harmful at this age—that it does indeed inhibit intellectual growth.

If the teacher is the owner of a private kindergarten which is operated for financial gain, it will take courage to adopt the fact that one half the applicants need to delay their kindergarten attendance for one more year. This means a 50% loss in profits for that first year (for one year only).

Many kindergarten teachers and many of the parents they serve have a deeply imbedded belief that early exposure to reading and writing will give the children a head start so they will have less to learn later on. It is always difficult to break down firmly implanted convictions even in the face of indisputable evidence.

In spite of these stumbling blocks, kindergarten teachers constitute one of the largest groups of educators who are insisting upon a revision of readiness and school entrance practices. Children at the kindergarten age show their unreadiness so clearly, it is usually of great concern to the kindergarten teacher.

READING SPECIALISTS, because of their training and their work role, might find themselves strongly committed to several beliefs which are in direct opposition to the developmental point of view.

THE READING TEACHER MIGHT BELIEVE:	THE DEVELOPMENTAL POINT OF VIEW IS:
that children need to be taught in order to learn.	children can and will teach themselves, especially at a time which is right *for them* and in a conducive environment.
that children who are not reading have something wrong with them.	*most* six and seven year olds are perfectly normal and might not be reading because they need more time to develop.
that much time must be spent on remedial reading.	that most of the work time should be spent on preventing the creation of remedial readers by using knowledge of the nature of human development.
that poor readers are generally caused by poor teaching or by disability.	that too-early introduction to the written symbol is the chief cause of poor reading.
that if children are taught the letters and numerals they are more likely to learn to read.	that children will rapidly and effortlessly learn the letters and numerals when they are developmentally ready to read.
that pushing, pulling, and enticing a child to learn is legitimate.	that since desire to learn is a natural human condition, it is best to trust each person to reach out for learning at the best time—that in fact pushing tends to have an effect opposite to that intended— it interrupts nature's

	timing and sets up forces of rejection.
that reading *is* education.	that reading is merely a *tool* which aids education —there are many other important tools of education, equally as important— *thinking—discussing—experimentation—manipulation.*
that there is a danger that a child might be ready to read at an early age and not have teaching available.	children will indicate their readiness to read by reading. They will teach themselves and demand aid when they need it.

COMMON EXCUSES GIVEN FOR NOT INSTITUTING A READINESS PROGRAM

WE DON'T HAVE THE SPACE.

The number of children you are educating is the same. Sometimes it takes a lot of imagination and creative thought to rearrange that given space to fit the needs of the children, but it is always possible in one way or another. Such "shaking loose" from the preconceived educational format is necessary if effective change is to be made. If your school has four first grades, two of them will logically become Pre-First-Grade rooms. If your school has one first grade, you will need some kind of combination, Pre-First with first. One interesting possibility would be half-day sessions for each group. (See section PLACEMENT ALTERNATIVES, pg.17.)

WE HAVE NO ONE TO TEACH PRE-FIRST GRADERS.

The fact is that at least 50% of your six-year-olds are functioning at a Pre-First-Grade level. If there is no one to teach them, then either they should not be invited to school or there should be replacements on the staff. Actually, when teachers understand what it is all about, many of them are eager to work at this level. Among those who are presently doing it, most of them have stated that they never want to teach at any other level. It is just about the most "fun" place to work there is.

OUR PARENTS WON'T GO FOR IT.

This is true. They won't go for it unless they are educated to the concepts involved. It is, however, most unfair of the educator to make the assumption that parents won't like the idea. Experience has shown that when parents are given the chance to learn about it (see section A STRATEGY FOR CHANGE, pg. 63) 90-100% become enthusiastic supporters.

"OUR" COMMUNITY IS DIFFERENT!

This excuse has simply not held up. Experience in various types of communities indicates that the *concepts are so basic to humans in general* that acceptance of a readiness program takes place in underprivileged, affluent, industrial, rural, and city communities. Also, the kind of community seems to make no difference in the degree of *need* for attention to school readiness.

WE ARE WORKING FOR KINDERGARTEN INSTEAD.

Actually, this is not a bad excuse. For many towns, it is a very sensible way to handle the problem. Usually, however, when this excuse is used, it is done with the idea that kindergarten will "get the kids ready for first grade." In that context, it is a false hope. It will not make one bit of difference in the number of children who are ready for first grade, *developmentally!*

A kindergarten can take the place of a Pre-First-Grade room—IF—the kindergarten is used for six-year-olds as well as five-year-olds. (See sections PLACEMENT ALTERNATIVES, pg. 17, and KINDERGARTEN AS IT RELATES TO THE READINESS PROGRAM, pg. 21.)

SOME QUESTIONS ASKED BY EDUCATORS

How do you get the parents to go along with this idea?

This is usually asked by educators whose school has been involved in a Readiness Program, but have not used a planned strategy in making this change. A carefully-thought-out strategy for change takes into consideration that the parents must be among the first people educated to the readiness concepts, and such a strategy will provide for carefully executed discussion periods with parents. Informed parents find the development-readiness concepts easy to adopt.

What if a child is only five years old developmentally, but is very bright and can read already and do first grade work? How can you put such a child in a Pre-First-Grade room?

This question reflects the educator's difficulty in realizing that there are more important things about human beings than their intelligence and that there is a lot more to learn in this world than academics. A Pre-First-Grade room will provide a stimulating environment in which these children will grow socially and physically and give them a chance to develop emotional stamina. There is much intellectualization going on in the Pre-First-Grade room and there are lots of library books to be read. First grade for children at this developmental level would tend to push their intellectual growth at the expense of their social, emotional, and physical growth, and in no time at all, they would be out-of-balance people.

You said some kids need two extra years. That means they won't go to first grade until they are eight. I have seen kids who have repeated twice and when they get to Junior High they are big problems. They are wise guys and are discipline problems.

There is a world of difference between children who are fourteen upon entering seventh grade because they failed two grades and children who enter at fourteen because they were eight when they entered first grade. Repeaters are angry, defeated people who, because they didn't measure up to the school's arbitrary standards from the beginning, have very low opinions of themselves. Their behavior reflects their experiences, not their age. Children who start out at age eight have a good chance of tasting success from the beginning. They are likely to arrive in Junior High with good feelings about themselves and about school.

What do I say to the parent who says, "My child has learned things in kindergarten. Now all he does is play in the Pre-First-Grade room?"

Again, it can't be overemphasized that parent education should *precede* all other phases of the readiness program. Part of this education includes an understanding of why and how "play" is children's work. It also includes the idea that learning "things" is not education. This education of parents also makes clear that when something is truly learned it becomes an integral part of the child's development. Therefore, if learning has been important to the child's development, it will not be lost.

Won't the children in the Pre-First-Grade lose out by not being mixed in with the bright children?

Here we go again! The educator, much more than the parent, finds it hard to believe that a child who is developmentally young for the first grade at age six can be intellectually brilliant. There is as wide a variance of intelligence in the Pre-First-Grade room as there is in any other grade. It would be hard to find a more heterogeneous grouping than is found in the Pre-First-Grade room.

PARENTS ARE PARTNERS
IN SCHOOL CHANGE

Change means moving from one spot to another. In this case, it means moving from

> using chronological age as
> a criterion for school readiness

> to

> > using developmental age as
> > a criterion for school readiness.

It is the responsibility of the school to help the parents make this transition. This is accomplished by three main thrusts: 1) educating parents, in small group meetings, to the concepts of child development as they relate to school readiness, 2) interviewing individual parents after the examining has been completed to discuss child's placement, 3) soliciting parental help in equipping the Pre-First-Grade room or in acting as volunteer aides.

EDUCATION OF PARENTS

To help the parent with the transition, the educator needs to know

> where the parent is now,

> and

> > where the parent needs to go.

THE AVERAGE PARENTS THINK:

what has always been done regarding school entrance is all right.

intelligence is the main ingredient of school success.

a child who can read is successful.

an early start in academics leads to more success later on.

children can be *taught* readiness.

all six-year-olds are ready for school.

children can be *made* to learn.

success in school is the most important thing in the world.

what children *know* is a measure of their readiness for school.

learning readiness and school readiness are synonymous.

children learn only when they are *taught*.

school people know more about education than parents do.

THE AVERAGE PARENTS FEEL:

wary about any change which affects their child, who is the most important thing in the world to them.

guilty if their child is not ready for school.

compelled to *get* their child ready for school—"What can I do this summer to make him ready?"

skeptical (at least a little) about the ability of the examiner.

insecure, unless thoroughly educated and informed regarding any change.

pleased and flattered to be made a part of the change.

coerced, unless encouraged to express their opinions

openly.

more secure with the old method of school entrance than with the new.

THE AVERAGE PARENTS WANT:

to provide what is best for their child.

to be proud of their child.

to know their child is happy and free of stress.

to see others smile upon their child with acceptance and approval.

to have their child out of the home by age six.

to understand thoroughly any change being made—to learn all they can.

to be supportive—to help out—to be a part of it all.

to avoid family stress. (Sometimes parents do not agree with each other on child's placement.)

THE AVERAGE PARENTS NEED TO LEARN:

the disastrous results of an unready child's entering first grade are not to be underestimated. (See THE OVERPLACED CHILD, pg. 3 .)

school success is defined as growth and development with enough spirit and energy left over for extracurricular activities—achievement without undue stress. Academic achievement is but a part of school success.

school readiness is much more than reading readiness. It encompasses the whole child and is concerned with social, emotional, and physical maturity as well as with intellectual ability. Ready children are able to *cope* comfortably and thus are free to use their intellectual powers.

maturity can be defined as growth and development which evolves *without specific practice*. Many factors of maturation, then, are nature-ordained and cannot be influenced by environment.

the first year of school is the most important. It is the foundation upon which all other education is built. Placing children in first grade before they are mature enough to really profit from the experience causes them to "shut off," reject learning, often for twelve years.

unready children do not "catch up." They may seem to because they push their intellectual growth at the expense of other areas of development (physical, emotional, social). A child may catch up as a student, but fall behind as a person.

developmental age is a functioning age. Since all of us have our own built-in rate of development, there is a large range in the developmental ages of a group of children who are chronologically six years old. Since developmental age is an indication of the child's level of functioning, it is a far better determinant of school readiness than chronological age.

readiness need not be instantly fed. It is only strengthened by time. Waiting will not hurt the child. On the other hand, pushing usually does irreparable harm.

children cannot be held back from learning. When they are really ready, they will learn whether they are taught or not; they will teach themselves and demand help from others. Learning is a natural phenomenon and occurs naturally unless inhibited by outside forces, such as too early entrance to first grade.

a range of two years in the developmental ages of a group of six-year-olds is normal.

boys are six months less mature, on the average, than girls at the age of six years.

an interruption in nature's timing occurs for many children when an arbitrary age for school entrance is set by law. It is equivalent to passing a law stating that every child shall erupt the first tooth at age six months.

at least 50% of six-year-olds are not ready for the prescribed first grade.

very few children who are six in September, October, November, and December are ready for first grade.

adopting a cut-off date for first grade entrance which allows the child to be as old as possible is one expedient which protects many children. Changes should be announced at least a year in advance to give the parents a chance to change whatever plans they might have for kindergarten.

developmental age is a far better criterion for school entrance than chronological age. Although an earlier cut-off date is very helpful, there will still be many children who need the protection of a developmental assessment and many exceptions to the law will need to be requested.

a developmental exam is a device for observing a child at a given time on the developmental continuum of life. The indices of the assessment tool may be shown and explained at this time. Parents feel more secure if they have some acquaintance with the exam. No harm will result if the parent is tempted to "teach" the exam to the child, for no amount of teaching can hurry the child's development, which is evaluated by a skilled examiner's observations of the child's behavior rather than the child's accomplishments.

the chief purpose of a Pre-First-Grade year is to allow all children *time* to grow—to develop from within—to become themselves in all their total humanness. It allows them a chance to become developmentally six in the best of environments. It is not a place to teach them "things," but rather a place for them to explore and discover on their own. It is a year when they can be themselves without the encumbrances of arbitrary standards. (See THE PRE-FIRST-GRADE ROOM, pg. 25.)

avoidance of written letters and numerals in the Pre-First-Grade room is not a "holding back," but rather a shoring up of a firm foundation for later use of these written symbols. Through movement and the manipulation of materials, the child attains an understanding of such things as mathematical equations, the basics of engineering, and various patterns of language. These understandings are stored in the brain, not on paper. Later, when the accumulation of data becomes too great, the written symbol will be necessary to record on paper some of those things which are too difficult to hold in the brain.

SOME STUMBLING BLOCKS FOR PARENTS:

The parent might be faced with a dichotomy of "what would be all right for my child now," and "what is best for my child in the long run." Those children who are borderline, that is, almost ready, might be put in first grade because it is expedient. This, however, is unwise, because it is flirting with trouble at the junior high, high school, or college level—especially the problem of dropping out.

An unready child might constitute a financial strain. Working mothers need their children in school a full day, not half a day at kindergarten or half a day in a Pre-First-Grade room. (Half a day is desirable and recommended for the Pre-First-Grade room, but at this writing, few, if any, schools have solved the problems surrounding such a practice, e.g., law, busing, etc.) Also, when attendance to a private kindergarten is the school's recommendation, this might be hard on family finances.

In some cases, strong emotional feelings can supersede reasoning powers, causing some parents to fight the school in proper placement of the child. This is particularly prevalent when the child is the oldest and is a son. Fathers sometimes get emotionally trapped by this situation.

Sometimes, families which pursue intellectual activities most of the time find it difficult to understand the developmental point of view. The parents might be professionals or specialists and might, themselves, lead a rather limited experiential existence.

The parent whose child needs two years before first grade will most certainly have particular difficulty in accepting this information. There are always a few children who need two years. They are often boys who were born in the fall and who, after waiting two years, will still be only seven-and-a-half chronologically upon entrance to first grade.

THE DEVELOPMENTAL POINT OF VIEW IS EASY
FOR SOME PARENTS:

Those who have had an older child who failed or did poorly because of youngness.

Those who have a friend or neighbor whose child found success because of a readiness program.

Those who subscribe to a natural way of life—ecology, natural foods, instincts, etc.—those who tend to let nature take its course.

Those who are less social minded than some. They do not succumb to a "keep-up-with-the-Joneses" way of life.

SOME QUESTIONS PARENTS ASK:

Is there a difference between kindergarten and the Pre-First-Grade room?

Yes. The main difference is the chronological age of the children. Kindergarten is a program for five-year-olds, while those children in the Pre-First-Grade room are six years old chronologically (although younger in development). The program, facilities, and equipment are very much alike if the kindergarten and the Pre-First-Grade room are both child-development oriented.

Won't a child who has been to kindergarten be repeating the program if placed in the Pre-First-Grade room?

Children do not repeat a program based on experience, movement, and materials. They learn from a piece of equipment that which is relevant to them at their developmental level. A child who is developmentally four will learn from a set of blocks something quite different from that which is learned by a child who is developmentally five using the same set.

If we have a public kindergarten, will we need a Pre-First-Grade room?

It all depends on how the situation is handled. If all incoming kindergartners are examined and only those who are developmentally five are admitted, most of the children will be developmentally ready for first grade at the end of the kindergarten year. If, however, children who are four and a half developmentally are admitted to kindergarten, about one-half the kindergarten graduates will need another year before first grade.

It is important to realize that, although kindergarten can be a wonderful and profitable experience for children, there are many aspects of development which are nature-ordained, and environment cannot hurry these aspects of maturation.

What if my child is placed in a Pre-First-Grade room and she suddenly matures and is ready for more formal education? Does she have to stay there all year?

Perhaps the most important part of any school readiness program is the teacher observation which follows the children every day they are in school. Teachers learn to "read child behavior" and gear activities to suit the child's needs. In some cases, such a child would be placed in the first grade room. In others, the child would be supplied first grade work without moving. The door is always open for a child to move. No one is ever "locked" into a particular group. One should always remember, too, that a ready child cannot be held back. A child will learn whether taught or not. There is nothing to be lost by underplacement, but everything might be lost by overplacement. Why gamble?

Do children in a Pre-First-Grade room feel a stigma?

Children seldom feel a stigma. Usually any initial feeling of inadequacy is strongly counteracted by the child's inner feeling of worth and of self-confidence which is developed by the Pre-First-Grade program. Moreover, it certainly would be counteracted subsequently by twelve successful years in school.

It should be noted that children's prejudices are learned from the adult world and that such feelings are merely a reflection of parental attitudes. Stigmas do not occur in schools where parent education has been well done.

Will the children "catch up?"

They aren't behind! Their development is normal for their age. The only abnormality is on the part of the school whose standards assume that all six-

93

year-olds are alike.

THE PARENT INTERVIEW

It cannot be emphasized too strongly that the success of the interview depends largely on how well the preceding step, the education of parents in small discussion groups, has been accomplished. The Parent Interview is *not* the time to educate the parents to the developmental point of view. This is a personal and emotional time for the parents and is not conducive to learning new concepts.

PURPOSE:

To inform the parents of the results of the Developmental Examination and to tell them where their child will be placed in September.

TIME:

It is more agreeable for the parents if they have two or three months' notice of where their child will be placed. Hopefully then, the interview will be in June, after the examining of the children has been completed, and the grouping has been determined.

PARTICIPANTS:

Both parents and an informed educator. The educator may be the principal, teacher consultant, examiner, teacher, or anyone who is well informed and interested. It is greatly in the child's interests to arrange this interview so that *both* parents can be present. News carried from one parent to another is often inaccurate. Also, it is good for each parent to have the opportunity to express feelings and talk things over with the educator. This cuts down on family stress and on backlash.

SOME DO'S AND DON'T'S FOR THE EDUCATOR:

Do set a time limit for each interview and stick to it. A

reasonable time would be fifteen or twenty minutes. Unless this is done, the whole task becomes too exhausting for the educator; and a tired educator does a tired job!

Do listen as much as you talk. Parents tend to answer their own questions and to become enlightened by their own verbal expression.

Do take a very positive attitude. Avoid being apologetic or defensive about the child's placement. By correctly placing the child, the educator is offering the child a million-dollar opportunity. Act like it!

Don't use the exam as a diagnostic tool. This is not the time to discuss, "He is strong in this, but weak in that area," etc. The Developmental Examination is a placement device, very accurate for school placement, but very general in its interpretation of the child's individuality.

Don't use the protocol of the child's exam to explain the child's developmental level to the parent. It is a waste of time and often leads to misinformation. After all, it takes the examiner a long, long time to learn to interpret the exam. What can one expect the parents to see in a few minutes? It should be noted, however, that the parents have a legal right to see the exam and if they insist, it is much better to let them.

Don't talk about another child's placement. Only the child of the parents who are present should be mentioned. Sometimes, however, it is comforting to parents to speak of the number of children placed in each group, "We are placing 53% of the incoming children in Pre-First-Grade rooms."

Don't use the term "immature." This word connotes an abnormality. Seldom is a child immature. Instead, the child is simply "developmentally young" for the prescribed first grade.

Do have the grouping worked out ahead of time. Be very sure of your recommendation for placement and stick to it. Being vague or apologetic only leaves the parent confused. However, if the parent is adamant, do concede.

THE ADAMANT PARENT:

If a parent has been informed to the best of the educator's ability and still disagrees with the school's choice of placement, it is best to sacrifice the child so that the total program will not be threatened. An adamant parent can sometimes stir up such fires of intrigue, hatred, and misunderstanding that the whole program could be impaired. It is best, then, to give in to such a parent. In doing so, it is wise for the educator to have the parent sign a statement to the effect that he or she (the parent) has placed the child against the school's recommendation. This paper should be placed in the child's cumulative folder.

Adamant parents are those who just can't bring themselves to accept this change in school procedure—not for *their* child. They often think it is great in theory and for everyone else's child.

These parents need to be treated with respect, kindness, and dignity. They are doing the best they can and they are doing what they think is best for their child. Their decision is usually an emotional one rather than an intellectual one.

The educator needs to guard against being defensive or angry when dealing with the adamant parent.

The incidence of adamant parents in communities which have instituted readiness programs has been about one in twenty.

DOUBTS PARENTS MIGHT EXPRESS:

When protesting the child's placement in other than

the first grade, a parent might use one of the following reasons:

"His father would never agree."

If *both* parents are present at the interview, this problem is avoided. Suggest that the interview be terminated and rescheduled at a time when the father can also be present.

"I don't care if she repeats the first grade, I want her to try."

Once children have been wrongly placed, it is too late for preventive work and they have become remedial students. Underplacement will not harm children, but overplacement can do irreparable harm. The educator might suggest that initial placement be in the Pre-First-Grade room, and then the child who does well will be placed in the first grade.

"He is very smart. He can read already."

A smart, but young, child needs to be protected from developing into an anti-social recluse or an emotionally unstable person. Most of the stresses in first grade are not academic, but are social, physical, and emotional. The child just isn't ready to cope with them now and placement in first grade will cause inhibition of growth as a whole person.

"We paid hard earned money to send her to a private kindergarten so she would be ready for first grade."

Contrary to popular belief, the purpose of kindergarten is not to get children ready for first grade. Its purpose is to give the child a good five-year-old experience, particularly in social growth. Although kindergarten enhances growth, there are certain aspects of development which only *time* can take care of. Doubtlessly the parents received their money's worth, for the child probably grew in social skills and emotional tolerance. However, this does not take care of the "youngness" which will prevent the child's progress in first grade at this time.

This is a particularly difficult area for the educator to handle, since the harm has already been done by a kindergarten which allowed entrance before the child was developmentally five.

"We can't afford another year of kindergarten."

This is another difficult area for the educator. If the school cannot have a Pre-First-Grade room, and the parents can't afford kindergarten, the only alternative is for the child to simply wait at home until next year This is better than coming to first grade too soon. Almost anything is better than being made into a remedial student!

"He will be bored if he goes to the same kindergarten another year."

If it was a good kindergarten program in the first place, this will not be a problem. The child will bring a whole new perspective to the same old set of blocks. Developmentally a year older than last year, the child will see everything in an entirely different light—the child brings a different person to the equipment and takes away a different set of learnings.

"She has a brother going to first grade next year. They can't be in the same grade."

If siblings are placed in the same grade next year, the resultant problems could not begin to be as devastating as those resulting from overplacement. Children seem to have much less difficulty adjusting to this situation than adults. Also, there is a 50-50 chance that the brother will be placed in a Pre-First-Grade room next year.

"I've always thought he was a little young for his age, but lately he has begun to grow up."

The acceleration in growth will not keep up indefinitely. Children develop in "fits and starts" with many plateaus and resting spaces.

"She will feel dumb if she goes to a Pre-First-Grade room. Her feelings will be hurt!"

Even if this were so, it would be equivalent to swapping twelve years of humiliation and hurt feelings for one year of it. However, children seldom feel dumb by being placed in a Pre-First-Grade room. They are soon caught up in high level intellectualization and mental challenge. Besides that, they have a lot of fun! They are glad to be there. Half their friends are there, too, and very often the other half wish they were!

THE PARENTS HELP:

In any group of parents, there is usually one able leader. Identify this person early and enlist him or her as chief organizer of parental aid, thus forestalling "hit or miss" assistance which actually increases the educator's work. To help this parent leader organize the efforts of the "staff," suggest group viewing of slides and films on Pre-First-Grade room activities. (See Bibliography.)

PARENTS MAY CONSTRUCT EQUIPMENT
  furniture for the playhouse area—sink, stove, etc.
  bean bags
    blocks (precision made—hard wood)
     coffee can stilts
     shelving
      tables (library, sand, water)
      wooden math games
       cubbies
        feely boxes
         plastic aprons
         peg boards

puzzles
easels
resting mats

PARENTS MAY CONTRIBUTE OR COLLECT MATERIALS
9 x 12 rug
wood scraps for carpentry
an accumulation of tactile materials—soft, prickly, etc.
factory discards of many kinds
discarded junk jewelry
library books
piano
dolls
furniture—rocker
dress up clothes
full-length mirror
sand for sand table
spools
cloth scraps, ribbon, yarn

PARENTS MAY CONTRIBUTE SOME TIME
to demonstrate a musical instrument
to hold a story hour
to take three restless children for a nature walk
to help transport the class on a field trip
to teach four children how to play marbles
to play a game of checkers with a lonesome child
to act as teacher aide one morning a month
to demonstrate a craft
to take three children for an elevator ride
to be an audience while some children perform
to teach the skill of sawing wood
to listen to a child's story
to wash and iron the dress-up clothes
to mend the library books
to take Polaroid pictures of each child
to bake cakes for a party

EVALUATION OF THE READINESS PROGRAM

An assessment of the program should be made each year. It would be unwise to plod blindly on with a new program without specific, periodic evaluation checks along the way. After the Readiness Program has been operating for a year, it is time to seek answers to some searching questions.

Of course the true evaluation of any educational program is an assessment of the adult which each student becomes. While we are waiting for the student to grow up, however, we can do *process* evaluations each year by observing how the student is progressing on the growth continuum.

Some of this evaluation will be objective and some of it will be subjective. The value of objective evaluation is quite questionable when dealing with human growth and behavior; therefore, most relevant evaluation of the Readiness Program will be of a subjective nature. Objective achievement tests are poor indicators of intellectual growth since they do little to test the person's ability to apply knowledge to life circumstances—which is what education is really all about. Information received from such tests is more apt to be deceiving than helpful.

Perhaps a rule of thumb in creating or selecting evaluation tools for an assessment of human growth and development would be to avoid anything which is cut-and-dried, black-and-white, labeling, mostly numerical, too neat, or based on arbitrary standards. It would seem that the most valid evaluation would be *an unprejudiced opinion based on observation of spontaneous behavior.*

Evaluators must create or choose their own assessment tools in light of their own school's program. The tools needed will probably change somewhat from year to year.

SOME QUESTIONS TO BE ASKED:

If the goal is to have each child ready before starting school, have we come nearer to it than we were last year—more

101

Pre-First-Grade rooms—more equipment in the Pre-First-Grade rooms?

Do most parents understand and favor the program?

Do most teachers understand and favor the program?

Has the number of retentions been cut?

What is the emotional health of the children affected by the Readiness Program?

Has there been good mental and physical development in the children?

Are the parents cooperative? Are they helping in the school?

Is the atmosphere in the school less tension-ridden than before the program?

Are the children creative or are they inhibited?

Are the children happy?

Do the children have good self-images? Are they confident?

Is there a lot of movement, experimentation, and creative questioning going on among the children?

Does the Pre-First-Grade room display the characteristics listed in CHARACTERISTICS OF A PRE-FIRST-GRADE ROOM, pg. 55 ?

Is the whole staff growing in their understanding and application of the developmental point of view?

Is the activity-approach, individualized type of program spreading from the Pre-First-Grade rooms to the kindergarten, first grades, and upper grades? Are the other teachers adopting this approach?

SOME WAYS OF FINDING ANSWERS:

Sociograms.

Individual, problem-solving tasks in each of the subject matter areas—science, math, language—posed to each child.

Records of the school nurse, with particular attention to chronic or psychosomatic illnesses.

Behavioral checklists for assessing emotional stability, social skills, and general adjustment of the children.

Checklists for parents, to find their degree of satisfaction with the program.

Measures of self-image—drawings, sentence completion, etc.

Pupil-evaluator interviews.

School records—attendance, referrals, retentions, etc.

RELATED RESEARCH

ASSESSMENT OF SCHOOL READINESS

Carll, Barbara, and Donald Randall. "Correlation of the Gesell Developmental Exam and the Anton Brenner Developmental Gestalt Test of School Readiness." Unpublished, 1971.

In an attempt to find a simplified method of assessing school readiness, i.e. shorter testing time, no special training for examiner, more objective scoring—the two exams, Gesell Developmental Exam and the Anton Brenner Developmental Gestalt Test of School Readiness, were administered to 36 Peterborough, N.H. pre-first-graders.

FINDINGS: Assuming that those who scored above the median of 65 on the Anton Brenner were ready and those who scored 65 or below were not ready, the two exams agreed in 29 cases out of 36, or about 80%.

Connor, Robert. "Developmental Placement Program." Title I, New Castle-Gunning Bedford School District, New Castle, Delaware, 1970. (mimeographed)

Correlation of the American Service "First Grade Screening Test" and the Gesell Developmental Examination. 140 pre-first-graders were administered both exams.

FINDINGS: The two exams agreed in 41% of the cases.

Contoocook Valley Regional School District. "Developmental Level-School Success Survey." Charlotte Carle, Reading Teacher. Peterborough, N.H., 1976. (mimeographed.)

424 children of the Middle School (4th, 5th, 6th grades) population were found to have been examined with the Gesell Developmental Exam before their First Grade entrance. Of the 424 children, 153 had been found developmentally ready for First Grade, 104 had been found questionably ready and 167 had been found

definitely not ready. Of the 167 unready children, 108 entered First Grade against the advice of the school. (No Pre-First-Grade classes were provided.) Comparison of the 153 "Ready" group with the 108 "Unready" group as they appeared in the Middle School years is very interesting.

1976 Survey of Middle School
Comparison of Ready and Unready Children

	Ready Group	Unready Group
Repeated a grade at some point.	4%	54%
Relates poorly to peers.	10%	50%
Dislikes school.	7%	44%
Been referred for Reading help.	18%	44 1/2%
Been referred for Psychological and/or Educational help.	6 1/2%	33%

Keene School District. "A Successful Start Through Gesell Testing." Pauline Jacobs, Reading Consultant. Keene, N.H., 1972. (mimeographed.)

A study was made of 222 children examined with the Gesell Developmental Exam in 1967 before their entrance to Kindergarten. Their degree of success was measured only in terms of their grade placement in 1971.

Results show that the odds are 83:17 against a child being in the expected grade if the pre-kindergarten maturational age was 3 1/2. It is 69:13 against being in the expected grade if the pre-kindergarten maturational age was 4. The statistics were much more in favor of those scoring a maturational age of 4 1/2. Here the odds become 72:28 in favor of being in the expected grade. At a maturational age of 5, the odds become 93:7 in favor and at 5 1/2, 100:00 in favor.

These statistics provide the evidence sought to support the theory that children having a maturational age of 3 1/2 and 4 on the Gesell Developmental Exam should wait at least another year before entering kindergarten, and that scores of maturational ages of 5 and 5 1/2 are predictors of school success.

ENTRANCE AGE

Hamalainen, A.E. "Kindergarten-primary Entrance Age in Relation to Later School Adjustment." *Elementary School Journal* 52: 406-411, March, 1952.

Study of 4,000 children to determine effect of school entrance age policies. Factors considered included home life, play experiences, experience away from home and others.
FINDINGS: (1) 24% of children entering school at 4 yrs., 9 mo., were found to have difficulty while only 6% of normal aged children had similar problems. (2) Under-aged children had more difficulty than normal aged children in all areas except the scholastic.

Illinois Association for Childhood Education. "The relationship of entrance age to pupil progress." (processed, 1960.) *Childhood Education* 40: 384-385, March, 1964.

Academic achievement (reading), retardation rate, and emotional adjustment were factors studied. Comparison made between youngest group (September, October, November birthdays) and oldest group (January, February, March birthdays).
FINDINGS: (1) Success in reading seems to be positively associated with older entrance age. (2) Younger children more likely to experience retardation in school progress. (3) Analysis of emotional adjustment yielded results not decisive enough to be of high significance. However, in all cases the percentage of students judged to be poorly adjusted was highest in the youngest group. (4) Differences between adjustment of boys and girls highly significant. Boys judged less well adjusted at all levels.

Connor, Robert, "Developmental Placement Program."

107

Title I, New Castle-Gunning Bedford School District, New Castle, Delaware, 1970. (mimeographed.)

Testing the developmental ages of all (152) of the incoming first graders. Mr. Connor wrote, "It is interesting to note that 86% of the incoming first grade youngsters who have late birthdates (Oct., Nov., Dec.) scored at the younger maturity levels (Pre-First, 4 1/2 and 5 yr. levels) on the developmental test, (Gesell Developmental Exam). The following chart shows how many children with late birthdays are in each group. It also points out the total number in the group."

Groups by developmental ages	October birthday	November birthday	December birthday	Total
Dev age 4 1/2		7	5	12 out of 27
Dev age 5B	2	2	1	5 out of 25
Dev age 5A	9	1	4	14 out of 25
Dev age 5 1/2B	2			2 out of 24
Dev age 5 1/2A	1		2	3 out of 25
Dev age 6				0 out of 26

BOY-GIRL DIFFERENCES

Ilg, Frances L., and Louise Bates Ames. *School Readiness.* Harper Row, 1965.

Sex and Group Differences, Appendix B. "----------clear sex differences in rate of development do exist. Our own clinical impression is that these amount to about 6 months in favor of girls around the time of school entrance."

Sabin, Carole. *Developmental Placement.* National School District, Calif. Report no. 1 - 70, Dept. of Education, San Diego County, Calif., 1970.

The Evidence. "For every girl in an educationally handicapped classroom (children with at least average abilities but unable to make normal progress or

adjustment in a regular classroom), there are *six* boys. For every boy in an educationally handicapped classroom born between Dec. 3 and May 31 (older group) there are *two* boys born between June 1 and Dec. 2 (younger group).
(San Diego County data)

RELATIONSHIP OF DISABILITIES AND OVERPLACEMENT

Portola Valley School District. "Developmental Program Evaluation." Curriculum Report No. 10, Portola Valley, Calif., 1969. (mimeographed.)

"The results show best, not in the subjective realm of more teachable groups, but in the actual number of children who are saved from educational disaster. Children who are started on reading before they are ready for it sometimes go on to remedial reading class and are labeled as dyslexic children or educationally handicapped, or as having specific language disabilities.

For children in the developmental groups, there has been a drastic reduction of such learning difficulties. The number of dyslexic children is less than half of what it has historically been, and, at this time, there have been no referrals for the Educationally handicapped or Remedial program from this group."

Ventura Unified School District. "Birthdate Study by Sex and Program." Ventura, Calif., 1969. (mimeographed.)

An investigation of the relationship of youngness and oldness to the number of children in various handicapped groups.
FINDINGS: In groups labeled: Educable Mentally Retarded, Hard of Hearing, Speech Problems, Learning Disabilities and Educationally Handicapped, there were more than twice as many boys as girls. Also, there were more than twice as many born in the 4th quarter (chronologically youngest) than were born in the 1st quarter (chronologically oldest).

109

Westlawn School. "Developmental Placement Evaluation."
Dorothy Hutaff, Educational Consultant, Fayetteville,
N.C., 1976. (mimeographed.)

After four years of a Developmental Placement
Program where the Gesell Developmental Examination
was used to place entering children, the following
statistics indicated these improvements.

	1972-73	1975-76
Number of children on waiting list of Remedial Reading Teacher	20-25	7
Number of Educable Mentally Retarded	16	6

NATURE-ORDAINED ASPECTS OF MATURATION

Connor, Robert. "Developmental Placement Program."
Title I, New Castle-Gunning Bedford School District,
New Castle, Delaware, 1970. (mimeographed.)

*Comparison of developmental ages of children who had
attended kindergarten before first grade and those who
had not attended kindergarten.*

FINDINGS: Of those children with pre-first grade
experience, either kindergarten or Head Start, 68%
were found not developmentally ready for first grade.
Of the children who had had no pre-first grade
experience, 69% were found not ready.

PRE-FIRST-GRADE PROGRAM

Roche, Helen. "Junior Primary in the Van Dyke Level
Plan." *Journal of Educational Research.* 55: 232-233,
1962.

Study based on assumption that a part of readiness was
a mental, social, and emotional maturity equivalent to
that of the average 6 yrs. 6 mos. child. Took place
within a flexible organizational plan called the Level

System, providing for Junior Primary A and B between Kindergarten and First Grade.

FINDINGS: (1) Children not ready for reading profit by being kept in a readiness situation until prepared for formal reading. (2) Moving children ahead into formal reading only after they succeed on the Junior Primary Level does not delay their school progress.

Haynes, M.L. "The Effect of Omitting Workbook Type Reading Readiness Exercises on Reading Achievement in First Grade." Unpublished Ed.D. dissertation, Peabody, 1959.

FINDINGS: No significant differences among those who had and those who had not used a readiness workbook.

Sheldon, W.D. "Research Related to Teaching Kindergarten Children to Read." *Reading in the Kindergarten?* Association for Childhood Education International, Washington, D.C., 1962. "Teaching the Very Young to Read." *The Reading Teacher.* 16: 163-169. December, 1962.

Two summaries (similar in studies covered and conclusions drawn) of recent research related to teaching young children to read with implications drawn for place of reading instruction in the kindergarten curriculum.
FINDINGS: "From the research which is pertinent, the studies and observations of 5-year-olds in a learning situation, and the evidence of the later effect of early learning, there seems to be little or no justification for introducing reading into the curriculum at the kindergarten or 5-year-old stage." Rather what seems indicated is "concept development and listening and speaking development in a comparatively unstructured environment."

Blakely, W.P. and E.M. Shadle. "A Study of Two Readiness for Reading Programs in Kindergarten." *Elementary English.* 38: 502-505, November, 1961.

Study of two groups (28 each) in suburban school in St. Louis County, Missouri, (year of 1959-60) matched as to age, taught by same teacher in same classroom in morning and afternoon sessions. Evaluated prior to experiment with Metropolitan Readiness Test, form R and re-evaluated in May with Metropolitan Readiness Test, form S and also New Basic Reading Test accompanying WE READ PICTURES (readiness book used). Experimental group had an experience program based on units of activity; control group used WE READ PICTURES. Limitations: small group, one school, measures of readiness might not predict subsequent achievement, teacher biased in favor of experimental program.

FINDINGS: Experience-activity approach resulted in equal readiness in girls; resulted in significantly greater readiness in boys.

BIBLIOGRAPHY

PHILOSOPHY — THE DEVELOPMENTAL POINT OF VIEW

Almy, Millie, and others. *Young Children's Thinking.* New York: Columbia University, Teachers College Press, 1966.

Translates Piaget's work into readable and useful form. Piaget's work parallels Gesell's work with emphasis on cognitive development rather than on perceptual-motor development. Will help the Pre-First-Grade teacher to understand the level of thinking of these very young children.

Ames, Louise B. *Is Your Child in the Wrong Grade?* Scranton, Pa.: Harper and Row, 1967. $5.95.

Tells how to know if your child is overplaced in school. Deals with the various ways children compensate for overplacement and what the parents can do about it. Discusses the "Bright Immature" who succeeds academically, but fails in most other aspects of living.

Good philosophical background to help in understanding the importance of correct school placement.

Ames, Louise; Clyde Gillespie; and John Streff. *Stop School Failure.* New York: Harper and Row, 1972.

Biber, Barbara. *Play as a Growth Process* (Article No. 4). New York: Bank Street College of Education publications.

Carll, Barbara, and Nancy Richard. *One Piece of the Puzzle.* Moravia, N.Y.: Athena Publications, 1977. $5.25.

A manual which emphasizes *prevention* rather than *remediation.* Recognizing that school failure usually does irreversible harm to a starting youngster, the authors recommend that as much expertise be applied to entrance to elementary school as is currently applied

113

to college entrance. It is recommended that children be placed in school according to their Developmental (behavioral) age rather than by chronological age. This is a practical book which offers a strategy for change to be used by parents and school personnel working together to assure each entering child is ready for what is expected of him or her.

The procedures put forth in this book are the result of five years of trial and error experienced by many of the schools which worked under the guidance of the New Hampshire School Readiness Project, a state-wide endeavor funded by the government from 1966-1972.

Very readable with a host of useful, practical suggestions. A guide for implementing a Readiness Program in any school.

Cohen, Dorothy H. *Learning in the Kindergarten.* Albany, N.Y.: The State Department of Education, Bureau of Child Development and Parent Education.

Beautiful kindergarten guide. Written from developmental point of view. Can give Pre-First teacher much insight into the inner mechanisms of children — how they think, feel, behave, learn. Excellent program ideas.

Cohen, Dorothy. *The Learning Child.* New York: Vintage Books, a division of Random House, 1973.

An excellent general overview of the developmental aspects of children in the elementary grades and the subsequent implications for schooling.

Cohen, Dorothy H., and Virginia Stern. *Observing and Recording the Behavior of Young Children.* New York: Bureau of Publication, Teachers College, Columbia University, 1958. Paperback.

A help to teachers who want to learn to translate children's behavior into terms of need. The very important and oft-neglected skill of recording behavior is dealt with.

Doll, Ronald. *Children Under Pressure.* Robert Fleming, ed. Columbus, Ohio: Charles Merrill Books, Inc., 1966. Paperback.

A collection of readings about scholastic pressure. Good background material for educators who are in a "selling" position regarding School Readiness.

Gesell, Arnold, and Frances L. Ilg. *The Child From Five to Ten.* New York: Harper and Row, 1946.

Behavior characteristics of each age as determined by extensive studies made at the Yale University of Child Development. *One Piece of the Puzzle* and the developmental placement program are outgrowths of these studies.

Ginott, H. G. *Between Parent and Child.* New York: MacMillan, 1966. $4.95. Now also available in paperback.

Suggests ways children and parents can communicate, allowing each to express real feelings without threat to either party.

Holt, John. *How Children Fail.* New York: Pitman Publishing Corp., 1964. Delta Books (paperback).

An indictment of common school practices that cause children failure and humiliation. Analyzes strategies children use to meet unrealistic demands. Very readable - diary format.

Holt, John. *How Children Learn.* New York: Pitman Publishing Corp., 1967.

Hymes, James L., Jr. *Teaching the Child Under Six.* New York: Prentice Hall, 1968.

Written from a developmental point of view. A very practical guide to early childhood education. Points out some responsibilities of administrators and the importance of working with parents.

Hymes, James, L., Jr. *Before the Child Reads.* New York: Harper and Row.

Excellent. Stresses the importance of developmental readiness and the folly of promoting such pre-reading activities as workbooks, rote learning.

Hymes, James L. *A Child Development Point of View.* Englewood Cliffs, N.J.: Prentice-Hall, Inc., 1961.

Ilg, Frances L., and Louise Bates Ames. *Child Behavior.* New York: Harper and Row, 1955.

Guide for parents. Excellent material for helping the parent develop a useful philosophy regarding maturity and readiness.

Ilg, Frances L., and Louise Bates Ames. *School Readiness.* New York: Harper and Row, 1965.

Contains the basic philosophy of developmental grade placement established through research conducted at the Gesell Institute in New Haven, Connecticut. This is a manual for the administration and interpretation of the developmental examination.

Jensen, Arthur R. "Understanding Readiness: An Occasional Paper, ERIC." Urbana, Ill.: Clearinghouse on Early Childhood Education, National Laboratory on Early Childhood Education, 805 W. Pennsylvania Ave.

Well written, clear report on importance of attention to readiness. Compares two points of view on readiness; the biological-maturational point of view and the stimulus-response point of view.

Kephart, Newell C. *The Slow Learner in the Classroom.*

Columbus, Ohio: Charles E. Merrill Books, Inc., 1960.

Don't be fooled by the title. Kephart enumerates the basic readiness skills which are prerequisites for ordinary school tasks. Part I contains a description of some of the major learning areas in the development of the pre-school child. Part II presents a series of performances through which the readiness teacher can observe and evaluate the development of the individual child. In Part III clinical methods for developing readiness skills have been adapted for use in the classroom. These include chalkboard training, sensory-motor training, techniques for training ocular control and form perception. A particularly good explanation of the splintered skill.

Lindberg, Lucile, and Rita Swedlow. *Early Childhood Education.* Boston: Dept. of Education, Queens College of the City University of New York. Allyn and Bacon, Inc., 1976.

A comprehensive guide to Early Childhood Education — *what* to do, and *why* you're doing it.

Montessori, Maria. *The Montessori Method.* New York: Shocken Books, Inc., 1964. $1.95 (paperback).

Many of Montessori's techniques and activities may be adapted for use in Pre-First-Grade rooms. Contains a very useful section on increasing acuity of the five senses.

Moore, Dorothy, and Raymond Moore. *Better Late than Early. A New Approach to Your Child's Education.* New York: Distributed by E. P. Dutton and Co., Inc., 1975. $7.95.

Part I reports research which supports the advisability of later entrance to school (age 7 or 8). It brings under one cover many diverse pieces of research hitherto unknown to most people. Assumptions made about Early Childhood Education are thoughtfully discussed

117

and alternatives offered. Part II is made up of suggestions on child development with emphasis on parent-child relationships. Various age groups are discussed from four aspects of development. 1) reactions that may be expected at this age level; 2) special needs of this age; 3) playthings; and 4) activities and opportunities for learning. A very valuable, well-organized book.

Pitcher, Evelyn G., and others. *Helping Young Children Learn.* Charles E. Merrill Books, Inc., 1966.

Suggests ways in which children learn and some materials that promote learning. Emphasis is on experimentation, self-direction, appreciation and awareness. Sections on art, music, literature, science, water play, cooking and carpentry. Especially valuable to Pre-First-Grade teachers is a section on academic preliminaries.

Radler, D.H., and Newell Kephart. *Success Through Play.* Evanston, Ill.: Harper and Row, 1969. $3.50.

"How to prepare your child for school achievement and enjoy it." Very good theoretical information and specific procedures for developing motor and perceptual patterning. One of the most useful books listed.

Rosner, Jerome. *Helping Children Overcome Learning Difficulties.* New York: Walker and Co., 1975.

While primarily intended for children with specific difficulties, many of the suggested activities can be used with the young child and help teachers to better understand the nature of perception.

Sharp, Evelyn. *Thinking Is Child's Play.* New York: E. P. Dutton and Co., Inc., 1969.

Divided into two sections: the first dealing with "how children learn" and the second, a collection of suggested games related to the development of the thinking process in young children.

PRE-FIRST-GRADE PROGRAM

Andrews, Gladys. *Creative Movement for Children.* Prentice-Hall, Inc., 1954.

Canner, Norma. *Children Discover Music and Dance.* New York: Henry Holt.

Carson, Rachel. *The Sense of Wonder.* Harper and Row, 1965.

Cook, Ann. *Cooking in the Open Classroom.* City University of New York, 1971.

Defines the role of cooking and its extension into various classroom activities. Includes recipes with pictorial representations of the cooking process and a list of related books.

Copeland, Richard W. *How Children Learn Mathematics.* New York: MacMillan Co., 1970.

David and Day. *Water, The Mirror of Science.* Anchor (Doubleday), 1967. Paperback.

deRegniers, Beatrice. *The Shadow Book.* Harcourt Brace, 1960.

Dutton, June, and Charles Schultz. *Peanuts Cook Book.* Scholastic Book Services, 1970.

Recipes children can use successfully are interspersed with Peanuts cartoons.

Dwyer, M. Christine, and Forenti. *The Child Will Learn.* Department of Education, Division of Instruction, Title I, E.S.E.A., 64 North Main St., Concord, N.H.

A program for developing language and thinking skills

119

with a collection of suggested activities integrating all areas of learning. Behavioral objectives are defined for each activity; supplies needed are listed.

Ellis, Mary Jackson, and Frances Lyons. *Finger Playtime.* Minneapolis, Minn.: T. S. Denison and Co., 1960. $3.00.

Finger actions to make in conjunction with little poems. ("Here's the church, and here's the steeple...." type of activity.) Very good. Develops dexterity, eye-hand coordination, correlates speech with action.

Ellis, Mary Jackson. *Fingerplay Approach to Dramatization.* Minneapolis, Minn.: T. S. Denison and Co., 1960. $3.00.

More of the same.

Feravolo, Rocco V. *Junior Science Book of Magnets.* Garrard Press, 1960.

Freeman, Mae, and Ira. *Fun and Experiments with Light.* Random House, 1963.

Fuller, Elizabeth Mechem, and Mary Ellis. *Learning How to Use the Five Senses.* Minneapolis, Minn.: T. S. Denison and Co., 1961. $3.50.

Excellent. A wealth of material. Many practical suggestions for classroom use.

Geri, Frank H. *Games and Rhythms for Children.* Prentice-Hall, Inc., 1955.

Golden Nature Guides. New York: Simon and Schuster, Inc., (paper).

Birds	*Reptiles and Amphibians*
Fishes 1956	*Sea Shells of the World* 1962
Insects 1956	Many others

Harrison, George Russell. *The First Book of Light.* Franklin Watts, 1962.

Hein, Lucille E. *Enjoying the Outdoors with Children.* New York: Association Press, 1966. $3.95.

Suggestions on how to introduce children to the outdoors and the world of nature and how to develop the use of their five senses.

Hull, William, and others. *Attribute Games and Problems, Elementary Science Study.* New York: Webster Division, McGraw-Hill Book Co., 1968.

Kleinman, Louis W. *Easy Science Experiments.* Hart Publishing Co., 1959.

Knight, David C. *The First Book of Sound.* Franklin Watts, 1960.

Lavatelli, Celia Stendler. *Teachers Guide to accompany Early Childhood Curriculum - A Piaget Program.* Cambridge, Mass.: American Science and Engineering, Inc., 1970.

McGavack, John Jr., and Donald P. LaSalle. *Guppies, Bubbles, and Vibrating Objects.* New York: The John Day Co., 1969.

Units include "How To Do It," "Balancing Blocks," "Measurement for Wee People," "Shapes and Structures," "Shadows and Sundials," "Topology for Tots." The ideas and activities suggested to motivate children are such that the classroom atmosphere is one of excitement in learning.

Meyer, Jerome S. *Prisms and Lenses.* World Publishers, 1959.

Minnemast Coordinated Mathematics - Science Series, Minnemast Center, 720 Washington Ave., S.E., Minneapolis, Minn.

*Watching and   Introducing
Wondering   Measurement*

Curves and Shapes	*Numeration*
Describing and	*Introducing*
Classifying	*Symmetry*
Using Our Senses	

Mosston, Muska. *Developmental Movement.* Columbus, Ohio: Charles E. Merrill Books, Inc., 1965.

A systematic approach to development of agility, balance, flexibility and strength in the child. Exercises and games are presented in order of difficulty to develop motor skills and coordination. Many inexpensive props and very basic equipment may be used either indoors or out. This creative approach to body development will delight young children.

Northwest Regional Educational Laboratory. *Coordinated Helps in Language Development* (CHILD). Portland, Oregon: Copy-Print Centers, 1206 S.W. Jefferson, 1970. $4.00.

Full of excellent ideas for teachers to help children expand their verbal powers and to bind language and thought.

Nuffield Mathematics Project. New York: John Wiley and Sons, Inc., 1967, 1969.

Beginnings	*Mathematics Begins*
Environmental	*Pictorial Representation*
Geometry	
I Do and	
I Understand	

Shulman, Anne Shaaker, and others. "Firsthand Experiences and Sensory Learning." Bank Street College of Education, New York.

Snyder, Alice. *Sing and Strum.* New York: Mills Music, Inc., 1619 Broadway. $1.25.

Song book with chords for Autoharp.

Sootin, Harry. *Science Experiments with Sound*. Norton and Co., 1964.

Talks for Primary School Teachers. New Rochelle, New York: Cuisenaire Co. of America, Inc., 12 Church St., 1964.

Valens, E.G. *Magnet*. World Publishing Co., 1964.

FILMS

The Activity Oriented Classroom, B&W, 28 min. Campbell Films, Inc., Saxtons River, Vt., Purchase price $125.00, rental $12.50. (Available to *New Hampshire residents* at a rental fee of $2.50 from Media Services, U.N.H., Durham.)

Film depicting a first grade in Mt. Lebanon School, West Lebanon, N.H. Emphasis is on learning rather than teaching. *Environment* is structured, rather than the children or the program. Excellent for teachers interested in setting up activity centers in the classroom. Shows a typical day. Produced by the New Hampshire School Readiness Project of Title III ESEA in 1969.

And Sow Tomorrow, Color, 29 min., University of New Hampshire, Department of Media Services, Durham, N.H. 03824. Rental $6.00.

Filmed at Toronto. An up-to-date look at education and learning and the direction schools might take.

Blocks - A Medium for Perceptual Learning, Color, 16 min. Campus Film Distributors Corp., 20 East 46th St., New York, N.Y. 10017. Rental $20.00.

Particularly excellent for verbalization of the learning process which takes place as child plays with blocks.

"Block building provides the framework for many academic learnings."

123

"Blocks as a medium has presented the children with a challenge to create. Building with a purpose, they have explored form, pattern and space. And although some of the structures are relatively simple, the learnings are far reaching and essential for their conceptual development. Thus they acquire knowledge which they will use as a foundation for the future."

Dramatic Play. . .An Integrative Process For Learning, Color, 32 min., Campus Film Distributors Corp., 20 East 46th St., New York, N.Y. 10017. Rental $20.00.

A teacher training film for early childhood education. Through live action, dialogue, and narration, the film presents the inherent intellectual, social and emotional learnings in dramatic play and the strategies used by the children in dealing with individuals and materials. The film further details the role of the teacher as an essential part in the total integrating process. The film was produced by Campus Film Productions, Inc., in cooperation with Queens College of the City University of New York, Board of Higher Education.

Embryology of Human Behavior, Color, 28 min. University of New Hampshire, Department of Media Services, Durham, N.H. 03824. Rental $2.00.

Takes for its theme the premise that the physical and psychological makeup of the child is determined by deep-seated laws of growth. The film extends the concepts of embryology to include the action system of the child as manifested in patterns of behavior both before and after birth. Demonstrated is the technique of developmental diagnosis by clinical examinations which bring into contrast children at comparable ages. Growth proves to be a key concept for interpreting the nature and needs of all types of children, whether normal or handicapped. For a detailed statement of this film and many illustrations, see Chapter II of *Infant Development* by Arnold Gesell, M.D. (Harper and Row, Publishers). The film was produced by the Association of American Medical Colleges, and narrated by Dr. Gesell, 1951.

Learning in the Kindergarten, B&W, (series of 5 - 15 min. excerpts). B'nai B'rith, 315 Lexington Ave., New York, NY 10016. Rental $10.00.

Filmed at Lexington, Mass. and the Eliot-Pearson Children's School in Medford, Mass. Five to fifteen minute excerpts depicting specific activities. Teacher training film.

Primary Education in England (British Infant Schools), Color, 15 min. I/D/E/A, P.O. Box 446, Melbourne, Florida 32901. Rental $10.00.

Setting Up a Room, Color, 30 min. Campus Film Distributors Corp., 20 East 46th St., New York, N.Y. 10017. Rental $20.00.

Two kindergarten teachers arrange the equipment and furniture in the kindergarten room while giving the rationale for each move.

Time to Grow, Color, 29 min. Campbell Films, Inc., Saxtons River, Vt. Purchase price $205.00, Rental $15.00.

(Available to *New Hampshire residents* at a rental fee of $2.50 from Media Services, U.N.H., Durham, and from Keene State College, Audio-Visual Department, Keene.)

Film of programs in two New Hampshire Pre-First-Grade rooms for six-year-olds. Filmed at Wheelock School, laboratory school for Keene State College and at Derry Village School. Primarily a film for teacher training, it depicts the curriculum in a Pre-First-Grade program for children who, at the chronological age of six, are not ready for the usual prescribed first grade and need an extra year of growing and developing before starting formal education. Produced by the New Hampshire School Readiness Project of Title III ESEA in 1970.

Water Play, B&W, 23 min. E/D/C Film Library, Education Development Center, 39 Chapel Street, Newton, Mass. 02160. Rental $6.00.

Five Head Start boys experiment with syphoning, plungers, tubing, and measurement while at the water table.